Hunting

Hunting the Edges

Richard Yatzeck

The University of Wisconsin Press

The University of Wisconsin Press
2537 Daniels Street
Madison, Wisconsin 53718

3 Henrietta Street
London WC2E 8LU, England

1   3   5   4   2

Printed in the United States of America

Library of Congress Cataloging-in-Publication Data

Yatzeck, Richard.
Hunting the edges /Richard Yatzeck.
160 pp.   cm.
ISBN 0-299-16304-0 (alk. paper)
1. Hunting—Wisconsin—Anecdotes.   2. Wisconsin—Social life and
customs.   3. Wisconsin—History.   4. Yatzeck, Richard.   I. Title.
SK143.Y38   1999
799.29775—dc21   98-48656

To Diane

Contents

Preface

I am writing in a slanting attic above a farm kitchen to the sound of wild geese. The geese are so low that, with the north window open, you can hear their heavy wingbeats. On that north window ledge is a hand-made Chinese checkers board, drilled, nailed, and painted a flat, kitchen green by Art Bloom, a Norwegian farmer who lived in Genesee fifty years ago. It was on his farm that I took the hunting fever, and his acres were the first "edge" I hunted. I miss him.

Edge is a central notion here. It is, for wild fauna, the open space next to deep woods cover where clover, berries, grassy browse grow. Hunters seek edge to find game. In another sense, edge is where the demands of white paint, civilization, may at times be evaded. Here hunting and gathering is still minimally possible. The deer return to the glades to sleep, the hunter to white clapboard.

It happened that my urban parents, both of whom used "farmer" as a mild reproach, were busy. Separated by my father's late schooling, World War II, and their utterly disparate outlooks, they had little time to raise a child. I was sent to the farm in my mother's home village, at first to be baby-sat, but I took to following farmers, who were also hunters, as a young guinea fowl will "imprint" and follow a brood hen or "cluck," no matter the generic difference.

Fat and nearsighted, totally lacking in that modern desideratum, self-esteem, I came to spend much of my life then in Mrs. Bloom's books. She had been a teacher near Ladysmith, and she kept her library in a glass case in the parlor. I have here in my attic a *Tom Sawyer* that she read aloud to her children and to me before obligatory afternoon naps. Art's heart was bad and he needed a quiet hour before the work of the afternoon. I can hear Mrs. Bloom's rendition of "You . . . TOM!" and feel the radiation of her love of books any time I care to remember. Certainly her library was the other half of my imprint.

There came a time when my parents retrieved me, when I lived in town again. I had books still—I lived, soon, in the Carnegie Library—but the outdoor "doing" of farmers was lost, the hunting talk restricted to barber shop visits once in six weeks. The active part of me pined for the rural edge. Whenever I could, and regardless of the interests of the Bloom fam-

ix

ily, I snagged a Cardinal bus to Genesee to lead the horse that levered hay into the barn loft, once to spend Easter vacation hauling out a winter's manure from the barnyard and, in October, to hunt with Don and Kenny Smart from just up the road. As school and romance — *girlin'* — took my teenage time, the farming part of things tended to dwindle. I had, though, found a job in a sporting goods store otherwise populated by hunting and fishing bachelors — or as good as, when the season opened — and my Genesee time came more and more to be concentrated on fall weekends in the rabbit brush. Even during college at Madison it was a rare duck or pheasant opening that I did not spend on Spring Lake with Don Smart and his brother-in-law-to-be Charles Christensen, or in the cornfields around Genesee village. The Ithaca shotgun in my gunrack here is a replacement for the one I sold to finance a college prom. Herb Horn, another Genesee farmer, made the four-gun rack of clear white pine.

Jim Lockhart, friend, editor, and professionally, historian, was raised by a handy father, and vents his physical energies on well-made musical instruments and furniture, or in the garden. A Spanish guitar from his bench stands — unmastered — in one of this room's corners. Jim was raised at home. I was raised outdoors on Bloom's thirteen-Guernsey, sixty-three-acre dairy farm, and the nearest I can come to that past now is the daily walking and the occasional fall and winter hunting which makes up the physically doing part of my life. Telling about it, as plainly and naturally as possible, unites my literary profession — I'm a teacher — with my doing life. I live on nine acres of my own, thirty miles from the small college where I teach Russian literature. Russian, probably, because it, too, is mostly rural in its attitudes, straightforward in material description, and takes as its goal the depiction of a bitter Russian reality rather than of states of mind or symbolic constructs. My second wife and my second pair of children live here as well and have taught me (with mixed success) to love puttering about the house or in the yard. Still, the Wolf River in May or a blue October day regularly pull me awash or afield, with a springer spaniel for choice, though I go gladly with any mutt who likes to range. Not having been raised to domestic pleasures, I tend to seek the edges, the meeting place of plowed land and woods, in crisp weather. Here I range too, always expecting Frank Buck's tigers, occasionally bringing down a slow partridge — which is a contradiction in terms.

The stories here are a record of this activity, more or less chronological, some previously published in the same or slightly altered form in mainly Wisconsin outdoor publications. They form, together with short explanatory bridges between them, an outdoor biography. The codas are meant to help the mixture cohere, become a compound, a single story.

Approximate composition dates are listed at the end of each piece. It would be pleasing if you like my stories, for they commemorate what seems to me a better, more concrete world which is right now in the act of disappearing. They will not teach you how to hunt or fish, though, as I have not yet learned those arts.

Almost all of the people, dogs, material things, and events are real. The arrangement, the concentrations of several days or several persons into one, and the changing of names at times to spare the innocent and the guilty: these things make up, I guess, part of my style. There is little overt psychology and symbolism, as little, I hope, as there tends to be in real life. Rather, I concentrate on plants and animals, rocks and weapons, doing rather than indoor pondering. Each story is meant to recount a short journey away from modern life, away from home, to the edge of the woods, and then a return to white clapboard and civilization, without which the woods might not attract. Through these small journeys my spirit has been restored.

My old friend Jim thought that an occasional townsman might try to understand these stories. The fishing pieces are pretty well self-explanatory, but the weapons, fauna, and flora associated with hunting may need some footnoting. I'm not as sanguine as Jim is about city readers, but I'll try to be informative.

In Genesee there was a hunting family named Whittemore. Their ancestors were probably Scots–Irish who moved to Wisconsin from the Appalachians. Their own redbone and bluetick coonhounds and the English pointers that one of the sons trained for wealthy clients shared the big dining room with the family at mealtime. The walls held weapons: an L. C. Smith double-barreled twelve-gauge shotgun (twelve lead balls of that barrel's inside circumference to the pound), various .22's (rabbit and squirrel rifles firing a single projectile .22 inches in diameter as opposed to the shotgun's cloud of fine shot), a Winchester .30-30 (again, diameter), the deer rifle of choice in those times. Other shotguns and rifles hung on other walls. The shotguns, heavy or light (nine or six pounds, about), were used with heavy (no. 2 or no. 4) shot for geese and ducks, fine (no. 6) shot for pheasant or cottontail rabbit. The Whittemore men talked of such things, and I listened reverently, because they seemed descendants of Daniel Boone or Kit Carson to me, and maybe also because it was 1939 and war was in the air.

In Wisconsin, in those days, cottontail rabbits and that showy immigrant the pheasant were the bread and butter of hunting. The greenhead mallard during migration and, later, when I moved north to poplar ("popple") country, the ruffed grouse and the long-billed woodcock became acquaintances too. The white-tailed deer, a relatively rare quarry in the thirties, found largely in the North, have become ubiquitous and even a menace to automobile traffic during my lifetime. Mostly, back then, we stayed home and hunted rabbits, but the Whittemores went north for deer hunting, comparable, I guess, to today's safari.

We hunted these creatures, after chores or on Sunday afternoons, along deciduous — hardwood — edges or fence rows which then tended to be grown over with hickory, red willow, raspberry bushes, and long grass, punctuated by the great elms that are now mostly gone. Tag alder, blowdowns (fallen trees) covered with wild grape or cucumber, young thickets of popple, and canary grass were the usual haunts of our rabbit quarry. Pheasants were found in or near cornfields or in marshy cover. When the daily chores were too heavy we would go out with whoever kept coonhounds, at night.

I live "up North" now (I use quotes because it is such a relative term). The forests and woodlots have more softwood: the coniferous white spruce, red and scotch pine, balsam, but also the usual hardwood, the various oaks, beech and ash and poplar, butternut and hickory and the beautiful birch. Again the game lives along the edges. Our main quarry tends to be the ruffed grouse that nests near or among poplars and often feeds on that tree's buds. We use pointing dogs: golden retrievers and English setters, or springer spaniels that jump or "flush" the birds into the air (though there is often little "air" and lots of tree trunks which, when shot, don't cook up well).

Finally, about hunting itself. A growing number of Americans see it as a barbaric, sadistic leftover from less civilized times. I think, on the contrary, that hunting is a relatively well-controlled example of man's generally and necessarily predatory nature. The good men who were my rural role models tested themselves, admired the woods, missed often, and sometimes killed and cleaned and ate their quarry in order, I guess, to continue that hunting and gathering way of life which they had learned from their predecessors. They were farmers who did their own butchering and saw the hunting as an extension of it. Few of us have such roots now and hunting will, I think, naturally disappear. When it does, I hope to have disappeared too, but not before having done a bit to preserve its memory.

Right here is a good place to admit that this book would have gone unbuilt without the help and encouragement of Jim and Mary Ann Lockhart of Pine Mountain, California.

Bear Creek, Wisconsin   R. Y.
May 1998

Hunting the Edges

Okauchee

A red barrel
marked the driveway
to the yellow cottages.
Downhill
past the garage with the old Reo
the lake began.

Off a stone wall
was a drop-off.
Big northerns,
suspended,
slowly finned.

The men
rowed out across the big lake
before sunrise.
After bluegills.
Then they took me with.
Then we used an outboard.
Then I went alone.

"Off the stone wall.
Find the drop-off.
Big northerns!"
I caught two, once.

Now the barrel's gone, the Reo collected,
the cottage burnt, the green boats rotted,
the outboard junk.

Off the stone wall
at the drop-off
big northerns,
suspended,
slowly fin.

Okauchee village, approached by gravel road, was just another gas pump burg. But that last stretch around the water, between sunny farms and corny painted shingles — *Done Romin', Stagger's Inn* — was electric with reflections of lake between cottages. Then we'd spot the faded red barrel and, riding probably in our friend's Buick — the one the reigning Grandpa defaced by striking farmer matches on the wood-grain dashboard — we'd rattle down the drive past the two "hill" cottages to the lake. The lake! An always new, foreign world for me. The pale water, the greeny light through ash leaves, the old Scottish terrier Tuffy's weedy aura, and the mystery, when we were, finally, out in the boat, of the huge, crusty stumps projecting below in clear, pale green. Quick fish, bass with lateral stripes like rows of portholes, maybe a sinuous northern. There were tales of schools of huge, saw-toothed garfish seen out on the "big" lake; we had to stay in the shallow bay. The two islands in front of Grandpa's palatial main cottage, one with almost a castle — "Hodges' Folly"? — made of cement blocks cast to resemble dressed stone. This larger island became associated in my mind with some relative's trading voyage to the Isle of Pines; there was a large map of Cuba between mounted, dated bracket fungi on the dining room wall. Shaded outhouses with shady graffiti, intoxicating to an eight-year-old. Real split bamboo casting rods with competent reels — Pflueger Supremes, the old ones — leaned against the splashy boathouse wall. Weedy string nets and a wicked gaff hook. The armaments of angling.

A genuine mahogany Chris Craft steered by a blonde girl in a red one-piece bathing suit delivered the mail to a stone-gray bucket nailed down at the end of the long pier built on black steel girders. At 5:30 in the long summer light the dads beeped the car horn through an opening across the lake, returned from work in town. Sometimes there was an evening scramble across the shallow bay to catch crayfish for late supper — they turned dull red in boiling water. I was glad to pull my toes out of the dark and weedy water of the twilight bay. We all sat around the dining room table and played hearts on the oilcloth. There was milk and devil's food cake after.

On weekends, the men mounted fishing expeditions at dawn or played endless horseshoe tournaments on a court uphill from the snug bungalow-shaped cottages — one for each of Grandpa's children. Their shouts, and the clang of the iron shoes against iron stakes, made me forever doubtful of quiet men.

The lake taught me what Paradise would have to be.

The river where I fish now — a good, northern one — can never be quite as real, as promising, as Okauchee Lake was to an eight-year-old. Maybe because it cannot evoke feral terror and the secret blood joy that goes with that terror when you're eight.

Not my own face in the water,
but the menace, promise of mossy stumps.
All the world's wonder was, is
finning ferally in a childhood lake.

March 1985

Just a Minute

In Genesee, when I was young, rabbits were the only game. There were a few pheasants, seldom seen, but that needed a dog. There was usually a covey of Hungarian partridges. You didn't get close enough to them in the corn stubble. Rabbits, then. But it was a long wait from dream to roasting pan.

Of course, my first hunting dreams weren't about rabbits. Waiting to be scalped and perfumed in barber shops I heard every step—and misstep—of the barber's deer hunting. (All barbers were, it seemed, bachelors and sportsmen. There must have been some causal connection.) It was there, too, in the barber shop, that I got to read *Field and Stream.* In those days there were stories of tiger hunts in Burma, Frank Buck, Hemingway stalking Cape buffalo: more carefully told versions of the barber's lies. Outdoor magazines were sheer adventure. They disdained both hunting methods and recipes. The death struggle with the grizzly was central. No one thought about how to reduce the furry bulk to burgers. In my view then, all real men hunted. Some of these real guys that I've since met in the field have shaken my early faith. Then again, some have strengthened it.

These barbershop dreams began when I was eight and could read. My father, no gunner but a fisherman, was with difficulty brought to agree that gun ownership might begin at thirteen. Five years is, in boy time, a Paleozoic age. This eternity needed to be speeded up, filled with something. BB guns! My friend Don, just up Highway 59, had a Red Ryder BB carbine. He couldn't always get BBs—this was during World War II—but when he could I pumped and carried endless pails of water to the Smart family Guernsey in return for shots at English sparrows, "spotsies," on the telephone lines. The sparrows weren't often bothered—the telephone seemed to work all right, too—but I did get used to squeezing off aimed shots. Of course, at that time the birds were fighter planes, Japanese Zeroes, and the Red Ryder was a Bofors antiaircraft gun.

During hunting season I remember watching my uncle pluck wood ducks downed with a Damascus-barreled double 12, but he was soon drafted. Then I followed Art Bloom, the farmer with whom I often stayed, when he stalked a cottontail he'd spotted in the frozen canary grass by the pigsty. He moved carefully, without hurry, and dropped the bunny with a .22 short from the rolling-block action rifle that lived in the pantry next to the washstand. I couldn't have followed an elk hunt more intently. Art, though, was not really hunting. He didn't go after rabbits unless they came to him in the course of a farming day. He had enough to do with sixty-three acres, thirteen milk cows, and six children. His luxury was not hunting, but the one package of "Twenty Grand" cigarettes at fifteen cents a pack that he sent us kids to bring him, once a week. Or, maybe once a year, in early June, he would sneak off for an hour of trout fishing. I remember a rainbow as long as his forearm. Usually, though, his old willow creel gathered dust in the garage while Art raised dust in the field.

Those five years of *Field and Stream* tigers, sparrow Zeroes, and watching grown-ups hunt did, finally, crawl by. The long, hopeless romance with the worn silvery .30-.30 that Jack Evans kept standing upright in a nail keg in his hardware store faded. Christmas 1946 I got my own bolt-action .410. I was *armed* at last. All Burma and east Africa lay before me. At least, that's how it felt.

Don Smart, the neighbor with the thirsty Guernsey, had by this time exchanged his Red Ryder for a .410 single. In that ammunition-poor time after the "big" war my mother somehow organized a modest supply of 3″ .410 shells. The silhouette of a goose crossing the full moon on that single box of shells gave me visions of glory that that .410 was hardly likely to fulfill, but isn't hunting mostly dreams anyway? Don and I set off.

Not alone. Don's dad Orly thought that a mite of oversight was called for. Orly took us, in a '34 Dodge that doubled as a truck on market days, to his uncle Joe's forty, a rabbit-rich hunk of kettle moraine country because of its uncleared, overgrown fence lines. That journey, at a time when joy-riding had disappeared because of gas rationing, that promise of untapped rabbit riches, was more than worth a little oversight.

Things started very badly. I saw geese and tigers behind every bush, throttled the unfamiliar .410 in a death grip, rushed to rouse the first cottontail. I had fired Don's hammer single a few times and knew how the bolt-action of *my* .410 was supposed to work, but in my utter excitement I left the safety catch off. Don's hammer gun had had to be cocked before it would fire. Now Kenny, Don's younger brother, jostled me as I held my shotgun barrel skyward. I inadvertently pulled the trigger. "Ka-blam!" And Orly was on me.

"Just what in Hell do you think you are doing, Dick?" That was the merest beginning. Deliberately taking the gun from me, Orly worked the bolt, ejected a smoking casing, seated another shell, aimed, and shredded the top six inches of a cedar fence post. Then he explained, slowly, clearly, quite graphically, that some important part of Kenny would have been similarly shredded if I hadn't happened to be pointing at the sky.

That was forty-eight years ago. I've done a good many foolish things since. I've run out of gas in a blizzard, out of water in the Grand Canyon, repeatedly even put bananas in the refrigerator. I have not always learned from my mistakes. But Orly's language, the utter intensity of a generally humorous and laid-back man, reached me as no other reading-out ever has. I've never, never forgotten to put my gun on "safe" again.

After a long, sweaty lifetime Orly slid my air-dried carcass off the hook. We started in to hunt, Don and Kenny on one side of the fence-line brush, Orly and I on the other. Kenny was only eleven, and so went unarmed—but Orly carried an old, worn singleshot .22 rifle. "Backup," as he put it, if the shotguns didn't do their business. Shells were scarce and, even in 1946, rabbits were meat. We fully intended to shoot ten rabbits—the limit—and stock two family larders.

There were rabbits. They ran directly ahead of us through raspberry canes and red willow. They ran sideways, out across open hay or corn stubble. They even came back between us. Then at least we knew that it would be dangerous to shoot and so, for a change, didn't waste our ammunition. Counting my stupid mistake and Orly's lesson, we had run through the box of twenty-five three-inch shells in less than an hour, and we hadn't made a single rabbit mother unhappy. We had certainly shot quickly enough, but every time we were rewarded only by a narrow burst of snow behind, to one side, or even, rarely, ahead of the bunny. When we were down to our last shells, Orly taught us another lesson.

We had just reached the end of an unusually thick fencerow, close-set young popple overgrown with wild cucumber. A big brindled rabbit shot straight out the end, ahead of us. Don got *his* last shot off first. The narrow column of snow dust, rising before the bunny like a blast of a depth charge, sent him right. My shot, an echo to Don's, brought the animal back to the left. He sped toward a pile of that variegated fieldstone that seems to make up 30 percent of Waukesha County. "Just . . . a . . . minute," I heard Orly mutter. He hadn't left my side since the start of the hunt, so I could hear him clearly. He raised the old .22, slipped the safety, took what seemed forever to aim, and rolled the rabbit just before it reached the rocks. Open sights. Fifty measured yards. And Orly, like Art Bloom, hadn't been, properly speaking, *hunting,* since before the Depression, seventeen years earlier.

"Just a minute." Ninety-nine hundredths of our troubles, it seems to me, come from haste. The haste comes, I suppose, from the years of dreaming that precede action in your chosen field, from the confusion of dreaming with capability. I had just been really flattened—Orly didn't know about *self-esteem*—for the foolish haste that left my shotgun's safety catch off. Now I saw—had occasion to really learn—the positive advantages of deliberation. Annie Oakley had nothing on Orly. Don glowed, and envied his father's "eye." But I think it wasn't so much "eye" as taking pains—endless pains—to reach a desired end.

If I learned to check the safety catch on the shotgun, that was maybe all I learned. I cannot claim to have even nearly matched Orly's deliberation, his careful pains. I remember that cottontail shot better than any shot I've ever made. At impatient moments, if I listen, I hear that "Just a minute" of Orly's, in his very voice, though he's long gone ahead to feed the damned bluegrass. I've even learned that Cossack hunters, in the Russian Caucasus, whisper, "In the name of the Father, the Son, and the Holy Spirit," before touching off a shot. Orly's ancestors? I don't know. I do know that if I ever reach his stage of careful, painstaking *doing*, I'll feel, maybe, as grown-up, as worthy of respect, as much of a dad as Orly was. As much of a real hunter, too, in the field—and out of it.

January 1995

Like those Okauchee pike, the brown rabbits running, Orly's necessary dressing-down, and the good shot bring back the taste of wanting to grow up *now,* grow skilled, grow wise, even. On another day when I shot hastily and killed a hen pheasant—an illegal bird—Orly made me carry it in my jacket, in vivid fear of wardens and disgrace, all that day. I have, since, waited for the cackle and color of a cock bird before shooting, have never again felt forced to tremble and pluck my quarry in a dark cornfield as I did that night. Few of my teachers at school were that stern. Few lessons have lasted so long.

Bub

I am not ashamed of the wren's murders
Nor the badger's dinners
On which all worldly good depends
If I were not human I would not be ashamed of anything
        —W. S. Merwin, "Avoiding News by the River"

We were drinking a Pepsi on the steps of the village store when Bub rode up on his bicycle. The tail of the northern pike on the right handlebar just scraped the gravel. "Where d'yuh get him?" "Saylesville pond." And he rode off, a winner. All the village kids wanted to *be* Bub.

His family was Pentecostal, not Congregational like most of us. The women let their hair grow and wore black stockings. But whatever jokes passed about the goings-on at the tabernacle in the marsh, no one cracked the smallest smile in front of Bub or his dad. They were hard-working farmers, muscular, and dead shots. Among the males of the village they made up quite another, even religious category. Whoever had seen Bub ring the bell on the roof of the one-room school at three hundred yards with his .30-30 didn't fuss about his ability to speak in tongues.

Besides, Bub and his family were *neighbors.* When they found the first wild raspberries in the bluffs, or brought a gunny sack of morel mushrooms home in April, they were willing to share their woods knowledge and their bounty. If the rainbow trout in Genesee creek started hitting in late August, they feasted, but then they spread the word. It was just after World War II, and though people were not nicer, they did tend, and need, to help one another. Besides, woods-running couldn't take up much of anyone's time when horses and hay forks made up much of the industrial base. Farm hours were, and have stayed, long.

Except for deer season. John Muir's notes in *Boyhood and Youth,* set in Wisconsin, assert that "only the less industrious American settlers . . . left their work to go far a-hunting." I would hesitate to call the Matlocks "less industrious"—their barn was too well-kept and full for that—but Bub did go north to hunt deer in November. (This was thirty years before every county in the state had a deer season.) And he did tend to return, as Muir says of a still earlier time, with a deer and lots of cranberries. Once he even brought back a black bear to hang beside his buck in the box elder next to their milk house. (We had a piece—it tasted like

10

rougher pork.) I would guess that family tradition, Yankee blood that the Matlocks brought to the village from New York State, made hunting a part of Bub's life. The more rigorously Protestant Welsh and Norwegians who made up much of the population denied themselves such frivolous diversions, mere "fun."

When I was fourteen and old enough to hunt, my pal Charles and I decided that we needed to go north, too. The trouble was, his dad and Art Bloom, for whom I worked summers, were Protestant and didn't hold with vacations that lasted a long weekend or more. "Who'll do your chores? And how'll you get there, anyway?" Bub came to mind.

He had, on free Sunday afternoons, taken Charles and me in hand in the matter of marksmanship. Using Bub's .22 pump we got so we could knock a matchbox off a fence post at fifty feet. The same teacher showed us how to drop a Basserino — the classic casting plug — in a two-foot circle at about that distance after a run of bright summer evenings at Saylesville pond. Bub just might know how to get us up North. Unlike most of the older village boys he lacked a taste for deviling youngsters. It wasn't Bub who set us to wait with a gunny-bag at night in the cornfield on the wrong end of a "snipe hunt." It was the Rollins boys.

"Well," Bub said, when we braced him over a Pepsi at the store, "I generally go up with the Rollinses. They're kinda wild, but they hunt from a cabin on the eighty next to my uncle's place. Near Butternut. You fellahs could go with me. You can tell your folks that the Rollins boys don't pull much when I'm along. The good Lord help you if they get you alone, though!" We didn't hear that last part. We could go with Bub! And we knew that our dads, all the dads in the village, trusted Bub, liked him, maybe wanted, a little, to be a woods-running Bub too. O.K., then.

We hit Charles's dad and Art for permission to go at the end of second-crop haying. We had done "good": We had outdone ourselves at chores and in the hay that summer and fall. Both men had noted this; probably they weren't too surprised by our deer hunting plans. They did hesitate — Peter and Mike Rollins had been known to disassemble a hay wagon, carry it up on the roof of a chicken house, and put it back together there as a Halloween prank. Still, Bill Christensen and Art Bloom did finally give in, knowing Bub, and wishing, maybe, that their principles, or village opinion, would allow *them* such a jaunt. "But," they both said, as Charles and I found out when we compared notes, "you two be extra darned careful around them Rollinses." We hardly heard even the unusual "darn." We'd be with Bub.

Deer season opened, opens, probably always will open — at least in our memories — at 6:30 a.m. the Saturday before Thanksgiving. Friday at 5 in the afternoon Bub and his dad picked us up with Matlock's wagon.

The Rollinses had a car, Bub's family didn't. It was only three miles to the store from Bloom's porch—I'd often paced it off on the way to a Pepsi. We were to meet the Rollins boys at the corners at 5:30. We loaded blanket rolls and our gun cases and leather portmanteaus on the wagon. Art Bloom, on the way to the barn to do my chores, told Bub to watch "them cussed Rollinses," and he promised faithfully. Then we were on our way.

The off front wheel of the wagon came loose—actually rolled away— half a mile from Bloom's place. By the time we had gathered rocks and a brace pole from the nearest fence to lever the wagon up, run to a nearby farm for a cotter pin to replace the rusted one, and reset the wheel, we were late. Bub's face was as dark as Charles's and mine were pale. His dad hurried their big Belgian team, but we were twenty minutes late at the corners. No Rollinses.

We had never seen Bub angry. His dad's quiet "Now Bub . . ." might have warned us. "Damn those Rollinses," and "crack" as his hightop boot struck the newly hung wheel. Then he was on his back on the ground, moaning some, and I was on my way to Doc Towne's for help. Bub seemed to have broken his foot.

Doc was gone to a hard calving miles away; he doubled as a vet (or maybe he was a vet, said some). We loaded Bub, calmer now, on the wagon, told his dad we could walk our stuff back to our place, and the Matlocks left to find Doc. No deer hunting for us.

Not exactly weeping, but awfully blue, we considered our situation— it seemed like our whole lives—over a Pepsi. There are no words to express the feelings of farm boys who have waited maybe ten years for their first deer hunt and then miss their chance. No words that we were used to hearing anyway. It *was* quiet on the store steps next to those useless gun cases.

And then the Rollins's '36 Ford pulled up. They'd gotten a late start, after a later night (they leered), and where was Bub? We told our, Bub's, story, and didn't really understand the roar of laughter that followed from Pete and Mike. "Well," said Pete, the oldest Rollins, "Ma likes us to have Bub along, kind of as an emergency brake, I guess—won't let us take the car if he ain't with, usually." The Rollins's dad had died when the boys were little, leaving their mother with quite a handful to manage. Pete peered at our guns and bedrolls and grinned again. "Looks like you fellahs lost your deer huntin' chance." We didn't answer.

Then Pete seemed to have an idea, nudged Mike, and said, "Don't you s'pose you're allowed to go just with *us*? We'll show you huntin', won't we bro?" Mike, a little slower, caught on. Charles and I, stunned by this chance, didn't. We piled in, quick.

The ride north taught us, too late, who we'd hooked up with. It wasn't that they made us buy the gas—our folks had taught us that that was right—but we had to buy their beer and chili, too. North of the macaroni line in Wisconsin, where people begin to put pasta in the chili, anything went, in those days. The Rollinses drank, sang—not hymns—and whistled along in that Ford in a way to make Charles and me huddle together in the back seat. The speed and drinking wouldn't have, in themselves, mattered to us. Kids our age didn't drink then, but we looked forward to such "manhood." When the Rollinses pitched the beer bottles and lit cigarette butts out of the windows though, we were disgusted. We knew enough even then to want our woods clean and not burned over.

Worst of all was the chasing. Two hours north on Highway 83, at a crossroad, a buck passed in front of the car. Pete wheeled the car right along after, on the side road. Mike uncased a double sixteen and pulled out a five-cell flashlight. The buck, unreasonably, kept to the edge of the gravel, fifty yards ahead of us. When he cut to the right to avoid a sign indicating another crossroad, Pete passed him, cut right at that road, and hit the brakes. Mike was out of the car, swinging the shotgun and the light as the buck leapt the road. "Wham! Blam! Goddam!" And the buck was gone. "Load up boys, we'll see another," yelled Mike, in the heat of his near miss. Charles and I just put our heads down and pretended to be somewhere else. Mike hopped back into the car, loaded double across his lap, and we reversed to 83 again. It was a mere mercy that we didn't see another deer. But "gutless" is the least that the Rollinses called us. And their next case of beer took our last three dollars.

At the extreme end of a very long time we arrived in front of the Rollins cabin. Four uncles had been there for a week already, "gettin' ready for season." There was a heap of ham and turkey bones in one corner of the cabin, a pile of empty Schlitz cases in another, and a line of peppermint schnapps bottles, some broken, sort of wandered between the two heaps. There were four double bunks. When the Rollinses threw their duffle on the one unused bunk, two uncles offered to share their sacks with Charles and me. Pretty numb by now, we just nodded. But hoped for some alternative. The smell of those week-old bunks would have sickened a water buffalo.

As soon as we pulled in, preparations began for further travel. The uncles had decided to show their nephews Hurley. (Hurley served, for want of better, as northern Wisconsin's red-light district.) It wasn't much of a drive. There were rumored to be Chicago B-girls up for the season. The uncles were baiting Pete and Mike much as they had baited us. "Nothing loth," as Walter Scott used to say, the Rollins boys took off with their uncles, leaving us to mind the store, police the camp—that dump.

We bedded down on the floor in our blankets after sweeping and picking up broken glass. We didn't sleep much, and hadn't much to say either. Where, in this pit, did deer hunting come in? Nowhere, that's where. But that didn't make for good conversation.

Let me make a plea here for our innocence. We weren't temperance, we sort of admired fast driving, the dirt in camp wasn't a lot worse than barn dirt. We hardly knew what "B-girls" were, but wouldn't have been much shocked if we had. Stock farming, after all, is hardly asexual. It was that automobile buck chase at night, the combination of hunting with drunken fun, that bothered us. We thought then, after years of dreaming over *Field and Stream*, that hunting was a rite, a rite of passage maybe, holy rite, certainly, though we couldn't have used, didn't know any such terms. What we felt, dimly enough, was that the usages of hunting had been wantonly violated. Deer hunting, any hunting, was not, for us, mere fun. It was to be done the hardest way possible, by the numbers, and certainly not on wheels and in a hurry. "Just what are we doing here?" I whined to Charles. "I dunno, but we ought to catch aitch for it," he answered. We lay quiet then.

At 5 a.m. the revelers got back from the sixty-mile trip to Hurley. They said that they hadn't partaken. They claimed that the B-girls were "too dirty." Then they went noisily, windily, noisomely to sleep. One hour 'til opening! As Charles and I were giving up our last hunting hopes, one grizzled, red-eyed but observant uncle stuck his head over the edge of an upper bunk. "Get your duds, get your guns, and when you're ready I'll put you on stands," he said. No more. No less. Everything!

In maybe seven minutes Charles and I were booted, spurred, armed. The uncle slid down in his red nightshirt, grabbed Mike Rollins's five-cell, stuffed bare, horny feet into someone's pacs, left. We followed. The uncle, full of antifreeze, didn't notice the brisk breeze but led along a browned ferny path, past the privy, through a sudden tag-alder thicket to the foot of a steep ridge, and lighted the beginning of a trail up. "This ridge runs north–south," he said, "and borders an open field and a slough to the east. We've got a west wind—Cripes it's cold [he realized]—but if you two get up on that ridge and maybe two hundred yards apart, you ought to see something. With horns, mind! Luck." The uncle was, wobblingly, but rapidly, gone.

And we sat. Six thirty, and a light pattering of shots, in that almost vacant country. Then two hours—days?—of nothing at all. To boys like us, expecting a reeking, swamp-baron buck, just like the magazine covers, it seemed like two years. Then, dimly, the sound of a *tractor*. In that field to the east. Then silence, then muffled clanks. Country boys, we figured someone was changing plowshares. Then again, Bub had told us that his uncle had mortgaged the farm for a tractor, to keep his son on the place. (It didn't work.) Frozen through on that windy ridge, Charles and I met on the way down to the field. We'd been shaking so hard, for so long, that we couldn't have held a bead on an eighteen-pointer.

The sun wasn't coming that day, but it was full light. As we walked/ slid down the east side of the ridge, we made out the bony frame of an early John Deere. (Two-cylindered, that model sounded like a drumming partridge as it started up.) Then we spotted the oddly squashed bill and tied up earflaps—dandyish on that cold day—of a checkered, red-and-black wool hat. Bub's.

Expressing no surprise at all, we absolutely moseyed over and waited for him to notice our boots and glance up. He finished bolting a second plowshare, reached for a third without looking up, and said, "Well, there y'are. Come to m'uncle's here when yer folks was worried. Have a nice ride?" He grinned under his unmistakable cap. Long before one size fitted all. "There'll be room back down on the train for all three, 'less you fell in love with Rollins' driving?"

We could only ignore this, but did ask about his foot. "Hurts as much as my dumb mad deserved, I guess. Can't walk down a buck this year. Thought I *could* help Uncle Russ, though. But you two . . ." He appeared to consider for a minute, for effect I think, now. He just *knew*.

"You two go over to that slough. The wind is turning around and, about eleven—when you think you really *need* a Pepsi—the Rollins boys and their uncles'll head north into their tamarack swamp. A smart buck'll soon be sick of *them*. Maybe come east, upwind, over the ridge and into that slough. Slough's about two hundred yards across. You guys should be able to cover it." He turned back to his plowshares. "G'wan," he said, over his shoulder. "Don't come back without one."

Charles climbed a white pine on the ridge side of the slough. He likes to hunt high. Height-scared always, I hunkered down in a wild blackberry thicket on Uncle Russ's line fence, just north of the cattails. Again, from maybe 9:30, we sat. Dozed, now. Dreamed. Might have fallen asleep. When a dry throat woke me, or the sudden, scattered shots west across the ridge—Charles, clinging to his tree and so, awake, counted sixteen blasts—I felt like it could be time. "Dick! Dick!" Charles hissed, fifty yards from me. "Here he comes, right down the ridge." I sure couldn't see anything. "Bow! Wow-wow!" Charles used his three shots, not having known how to take the plug out of his father's shotgun. (Neither family owned a deer rifle.) I saw the smoke around his pine, then Charles, waving an arm: "Right . . . at . . . you!" he screeched. And then "Oh, Joshuay!" and he swung behind his pine's trunk, into safety. I finally saw why. The head and shoulders of a buck appeared, close enough, long enough to make out odd, palmate horns, right in line with Charles's tree. He'd overshot three times, not holding on the knees, as you must when shooting from up. "Wow-wow." Past me, at maybe forty feet, and into the slough, respectively. One slug left in Art's Ithaca. "Dick!" yells the reappeared Charles.

"Cripes, Dick!" "Wow!" And the buck went down in two feet of water. Up again. A leap. Single "ka-wow" from Charles, who had finally managed to reload. The buck went down for good. Silence, then "Hoo-eee!" from Charles. We sat a minute, after Charles had climbed down, walked over. His buck, but I had a hand in it. We flipped to see who'd wade into the slough. I went. Deer drag well in water. Charles gutted, though. I sat and shook—with cold and adrenaline at once.

Then to the plowing, and a short wait for Bub. "I thought maybe," he said, when he'd stopped the Deere. And no more.

We retrieved our stuff from Rollins's cabin—they meant to stay 'til they'd hung one up—and went home on the train. The buck, our buck, bagged in a tarp, rode in the baggage car. Charles's dad and Art met us at the depot with a team and we drove to the village, to the store, which shared a building with a tavern and dance hall. They bought us Pepsis, Bub they bought a beer. At Christmas we mailed a two-foot homemade sausage to that grizzled Rollins uncle.

Twenty years later the Rollinses were in real estate. Bub, having lost the farm, was leasing it from them, hunting squirrel, finding morels in the spring. Mike Rollins broke the lease, sold the farm for a mall site. He did offer apologies: "I need the money quick, Bub." "Yeah, well . . . ," said that dark face.

As the beautiful wood-pegged barn burned, he sat on the bluff half a mile away. His duffle, and his gun case, lay in the ferns beside him. "She won't make a Countree Antique Shoppe now." "Nope," I said. "See yuh," and he was gone down the bluff.

In October that year I got a card from Anchorage. It said, "No morels." That's all. Damn and blast the Rollins boys and all such!

March 1994

In this story the trip north, the Rollins's raw banditry, Bub's life and fate, are close to experience. I hear the low hoot of the Genesee train, the placid pacing of the big horses, many a morning before waking. The palmate horns of Charles's deer hang here in my attic. We got 'im. Joshuay!

Maybe my savage dislike of the Rollinses needs clarification. I believe that human beings are predators, but the kind of predation involved in land speculation gravels me because the bankruptcy laws make it safe for the predator. And then, the use of farmland as a commodity, when it is really life blood, accumulated sweat, love, seems particularly nasty. I once watched an ancient beekeeper weep. He had been swindled of hives and bees by a Rollins type who traded the bees for a car, smashed the car, and then forgot the whole episode; that is, he took the beekeeper's livelihood and avoided payment.

The Real Buck

His name was Bob Waidlich and he was in graduate school because he found Shakespearian English almost as tasty as venison. He was not a common type at the University of Wisconsin in the early sixties. Mostly, graduate students in literature had just stopped turning Catholic in emulation of T. S. Eliot and had begun to be nauseated by the absurdity of existence with Jean-Paul Sartre. If pressed for convictions, Bob believed in iron sights and straight bourbon. Otherwise, he made clear lecture notes and spent his free time in the oak woods and cornfield edges with a red dog, or at his kitchen table with a pretty wife and twin sons. He hit me like a fresh breeze on a hot, muggy day. Weather comin'.

We probably met over a bag lunch in the student Union, a daily philosophy session which had just then turned existential–gloomy. I was up to my eyes in Russian literary criticism, feeling airless and pointless, suffocating over an endless dissertation. I can see Bob that fall, scraping out an old brown pipe with a bone-handled knife, snorting the tenth time the power word "authentic" came by and then snarling, sort of gaily, "Let's go kill something!" I don't know if our eyes met by accident or not, but I was soon in his old VW bug ("They're not broke in for the first 150,000 miles") heading for the rented bungalow on a Wisconsin tobacco farm that he called home.

His wife Jane was airing the babies in the yard, hanging wash, and neatly avoiding the slavish attentions of the only laid-back Irish setter I've ever come to know. No snappiness, no wild surprise, just a steady nose and lots of heart in Jukes. *He* didn't find trees absurd, or birds either.

Bob and I drank a couple of beers with Jane, each of us taking one of the twins "tritty-trot to market" on a spare knee, then checked out the tobacco barns and Ernie, the farmer. Filter cigarettes had just become popular and Dane County tobacco, used until then for wrapping second-rate cigars, had gone up in value as a cigarette source. Ernie told us all about the hand harvesting, the firing sheds, the mainly physical work that tobacco cost, meant. Then he sent us away with grunted permission to hunt his one hundred sixty acres of rolling ridge land in that oak and granite country. The landscape was definitely lacking in theory.

It was such a relief. I'd grown up on a farm mostly, hunted rabbits

18

some, found myself in college because books suited my nearsighted taste better than football or the foundries where I worked in the summers. Now, in graduate school, I was losing altitude, weighed down with abstractions. Bob said, "Yatzeck, I asked you home because you never once said 'authentic' but always 'real,' even when that spoiled their argument. I thought you might like Jukes and maybe even own a shotgun." I did. And we hunted.

Every Wednesday afternoon, six chill, bright blue weeks of that October and early November we hunted pheasants and Hungarian partridge along the corn edges that separated the small plots of Ernie's tobacco allotment, or I hunted alone if Bob got a chance to teach as a substitute at the nearby country school. He trusted me with his dog and Jukes trusted me too. We got a bird now and then, and an awful lot of nice azure weather. My grad school megrims began to dissipate some. Then, a week before Thanksgiving, Bob said, "Next week is deer season." "I know," I replied, "but I've no place to go. Went once, when I was fourteen. I'm a small-game type." "Well," Bob said, "we'll go home to Hazel and hunt the bluffs. I *do* have a place to go." "Who's Hazel?" "My mother, but we're friends, so she's Hazel. Hazel's the librarian in Black River Falls and she's translated the New Testament into Chippewa. I'd like to be as in love with my work as she is." For Bob there was no higher praise, no greater happiness imaginable.

We set out for Hazel's, driving northwest in the VW, on the Friday afternoon before season. A couple of inches of snow were predicted, I'd borrowed a Winchester .30-30, and the VW's heater still functioned some. Nothing could have been better. The snow was falling already in the driftless area, that part of Wisconsin not flattened by the last glacier, and the conifers and whiteness set a serious hunting mood. Snow and pine needles. Real things.

Hazel. The wood stove was "hot as Dutch love." Coaxing a small town to support a library was like "rolling logs without calks." She had an alto voice and cursed in Chippewa. Alive and vibrant as the hummingbird that buzzed me once on the Wolf River. I thought it the mother of all yellowjackets and almost jumped in to escape. And what Hazel said, about Chippewa, about the poetry of it, and since it was 8:30, about a stew of home-canned beef and homegrown potatoes, was tasty. Nourishing. Hazel was not depressed, and just a few rods beyond "authentic." Bob had a real foundation.

Opening day breakfast, at 4:00 a.m., was solid, too. Two eggs easy over, dark sourdough bread and hash browns with crisp cuts of Canadian bacon on the side. Lots of black coffee. Then into the VW, gun cases angled in the back seat, coffee thermos erect between Bob and me, and Hazel's "Good hunting!" from the porch.

Deer season means, I'm afraid, more than Christmas to Wisconsin hunters. It means a return to the North, it connects us again with life as it was—or is said to have been—a hundred, a hundred and fifty years ago. White spruce, red pine, glacier-dropped boulders, the incense of wood smoke, the nitrous tang of gunpowder, "Daylight in the swamp!" and flapjacks. Every factory hand I ever worked with planned to buy a resort and retire "up North." Now this logging, fur-trading past had nothing to do with me, the son of Czech and Scots immigrants who didn't hit Wisconsin 'til 1880. Bob, I gathered, though I never knew what his father had been or done, was a rightful heir to this mythical patrimony. Not a spoiled heir, though.

We parked the little car on the sloping edge of the logging road—narrow by definition—and hiked toward the river bluffs. (Bob did, anyway. I couldn't see my hand before my face and dutifully followed Bob's rustlings.) Hiked and hiked. Didn't stop for coffee. Had to make it by first light. Bob, who was limber enough to climb trees, sat pear-shaped me in a fence corner with my back to the woods and disappeared upward along the brushy bluff. Not even an appointment for noon lunch, though I had another small thermos in my pocket and a couple of Hazel's sandwiches—bologna and sauerkraut on rye slabs, in a haversack at my feet. Hazel's sandwiches weren't pocket-sized.

After light. The wind blew across a rocky pasture into my face. Anything that passed there would not smell me. Northeast wind. All of Wisconsin, and imagined herds of unseen whitetails, spread east to Lake Michigan before me. I was finally deer hunting again, "posting" for deer, up North. Anything . . . lynx, bear, bobcat, granddaddy swampbuck . . . could happen. Really.

Deer hunting and, for me, any kind of hunting, involves a shutting off of the theory ducts, a minute and immediate attention to the only actual. I waited in that fence corner, squinted into the sun across that white, rocky field, like a trip-wired howitzer. I was, for the first three hours, all "shoot." But nothing ran. I heard shots, desultory, behind me and too far for Bob. I had, as we all have had, chickadees perch on my rifle muzzle as I braced my back against a cedar stump. I heard the ticking of downy woodpeckers, and once the uzi yowl of a big pileated. Twice tundra swans—we called them whistling swans then—swung high across my pasture. But nothing *ran*.

At noon I broke open the first of Hazel's sandwiches, cutting off bites with my otherwise unnecessary hunting knife. I relaxed my back with a good stretch, put the borrowed .30-30 aside (I had clutched it all morning), and poured a cup of coffee. Then, of course, the deer came.

Next fence line over, right before me and one hundred fifty yards away—no impossible rifle shot—the seemingly flat, dun silhouettes of eleven big and little four-legged creatures crossed from right to left, south to north. I dropped the morsel of sandwich and the knife to grab the gun and tipped over the thermos. Saved the thermos and went for the rifle again. Somehow managed to knock my binoculars against the one taut old fence wire and enmesh myself, jerking my head back like a horse with a skunk in the manger. Leveled the rifle finally to realize that I couldn't see any horns. Buck only season! Then saw horns, but on the one deer, near the end of the group, that was screened by two does. Lowered the rifle, sweating. And they trotted out of sight.

I was not, I remember, mainly grieved by the lost shot. I was, rather, amazed again, as with Charles fifteen years—an eon—before, that Virginia whitetails really existed, that what I had dreamed of, then, for twenty seasons, had heard the farmers in Genesee talking about in the long autumns of childhood, were real, flesh and blood creatures. This was long before deer had become the traffic nuisance and danger that they are, now, throughout the state. I was amazed at the luck that had brought them past me, flat dark brown against the new, white snow, numerous and joyous and alive.

> Oh, the rising of the sun
> And the running of the deer . . .

I thought. Now let's really hunt.

That glimpse of the presence of the deer had to last all afternoon, until almost closing time. Then something quick broke brush behind me, fifty yards up the bluff, snorted like a small steam train, and whisked on south. I assumed "deer" but saw nothing. The sun was behind the bluff, I had turned slowly to avoid spooking whatever it was. It must have caught my scent. Then, in maybe a quarter of an hour, 4:00 with closing at 4:30, Bob appeared and snorted too. "Come on, we've got a track."

Then we tracked, following bright blood on the fresh snow, sometimes close enough to see a brown back ahead of us. It had passed Bob too well screened by red alder to be identified. Then he caught the wicked half-moon flash of horns as the buck angled into a patch of sun on the bluff. Slow-moving just then, it begged to be followed. When followed, it explained its slow movement with bubbly lung-shot blood. Now Bob meant to "finish it, gut it, and hang it up."

Six fences, three good-sized woodlots later, we came up on him. On his side, legs stretched fore and aft, bled out running, dead. Still warm, a treat for cold hands. A handsome, squarish eight-pointer. We admired him, standing quietly, as even the worst of hunters often do. Then Bob said, "Get out your knife. Time you learned to gut one."

A too long time passed poking gingerly at the flat, white belly, 'til Bob took my wrist, positioned it just below the ribs, and said, "In two inches, then back it out to slice the hide right to between the back legs. Don't cut the stomach open." I sliced. It worked. Then hauled out unbroken stomach and entrails. Onto the snow. Food for the foxes. Circled sex organs and anus with the still sharp knife and the whole package came free. Sliced out the drum-head diaphragm and dove for heart and lungs, but the buck lay on a good slope and we could pour out the little blood left without much fuss, then rinse the cavity with fresh snow. How well put together a deer is! We put heart and liver in a plastic bag and laid them to one side. "How'll we carry him?" I asked, washing hands and arms in snow.

"When I said I'd hang him up, I meant here," said Bob. "Not our buck."

"But, but . . . O.K., why did I clean him then?"

"Because you'd want someone to save *your* buck if you shot one and it was too late to track him. We'll leave him here, hung up in this birch so he'll drain and cool out. Just catch his head in that crotch. Then, tomorrow, if the hunter tracks him, he won't be gnawed or spoiled."

"Oh," I said. I'd wanted the buck, thought I'd earned him with the very first major operation I'd ever performed, and I felt a bit grumpy.

"But," said Bob, then, "we *will* bring a toboggan with us tomorrow. At noon, if no one's come to get him, we'll just take him along when we head back for Madison. If the guy who shot him can't take the trouble to look for blood sign, or track in this new snow, he doesn't deserve him."

"Yes! Yes!" I would have said, with two thumbs up, if this had been the nineties. But it was 1962, and I just said "O.K.!" again. And we headed back for Hazel's, utterly lacking in existential gloom, full of the warmly selfish hope that the deer's slayer was shiftless or ignorant. We took the heart and liver with us.

That night, over fresh liver and onions and bacon—which goes very well with burgundy—Hazel talked about Chippewa, the taste and smell of campfire smoke, deerskin and the self-sufficiency that it meant for her, its nearness to blackberries, flint, and hawk feathers. Hazel did not look forward to heaven, nor was she downcast about its possible nonexistence. She lived *here*. She was as solid as those eleven deer I'd seen, as joyous, as at home.

Early again the next morning we parked a bit farther down the slope from the same logging road. Traffic and melt had taken the edge off yesterday's road. Hiked the same route, purposely avoiding the buck in the birch tree, and occupied the same stands. We enjoyed the quiet, but saw no shootable deer. I did see a doe and her two fawns catch my scent and drop to a crouch eighteen inches off the ground, creep past me in this posture that I would have thought physically impossible, and then disappear up the bluff. And a better hunter than I, a Cooper's hawk, nailed a red squirrel foolish enough to cross the open pasture. There really was enough going on to put deerslaying on the back burner 'til next year. Noon came.

I noticed that Bob, however laudable his ethics, really moved with that toboggan as we approached the—I almost said *our*—buck. And the buck was there—no tracks near but ours—and not gnawed either. Onto the toboggan, turn and turn about pulling, and back to the VW. We *had* tagged him first. Now he *was* ours.

By noon it was an even warmer day, the VW had settled with the snow further into the roadside mud, and with the buck on top, and even one of us inside to drive, the little car didn't care to move. We tried to push it out but got hung up on the heater boxes. Now what? But a pickup with three fairly sober buddies pulled up, offered to pull us out "for a buck," then we all just lifted and shoved the car, buck and all, back up on the logging road. On the way back to Madison we were a special attraction for little boys in small towns. A buck, *any* buck, looks mighty big on the top of a VW. Basta!

So now, thirty-some years later, just last week, I was brown-bagging it in the faculty lounge. A young colleague, new boy at our mini-college, was spicing his harangue with words like "empowerment," "valorization," and even "deconstruction." Over and through the heavy voltage of these words, I also, clearly though distantly, heard the phrase, "Let's go kill something!" and had a powerful sensation of Sir Walter Raleigh, though no one in our lounge smokes a pipe. I nodded politely, picked up my brown bag, and headed for my rusty Honda. I haven't seen Bob in thirty years. Still, I had the feeling of "weather comin'!"

January 1993

The critical theory of graduate-school literary studies, as opposed to the real texts, was a grinding dullness for me. Occasional hunts, Renaissance music on Friday nights, got me through — rather slowly. "Waidlich," reading this piece, remembered that the sharp crust on the snow skewed his balance, hindered his haste toward the one good hunting spot. I remember the unarguable weight of the deer swung up in the tree, Hazel's amazingly black eyes, and the fierce beauty of the Cooper's hawk against the snow.

Esther's Ducks

Jolting north in Christensens' pickup after high school graduation, hung over from pretty Audrey's father's sloe gin, I muttered, "Thus conscience does make cowards of us all." I thought I'd made up the line. Charles just said, "Bull! All you need is some fishin'!" And he was right, as he has mostly been, since I've known him. (*You've* known him to shoot a buck, in "Bub.") We got a good mess of northern pike, and even some turtles (who had eaten the pike) on that trip.

Then, ten years later, I was helping Charles and his mother Esther (who hates to be called Essie) gather bales on a ten-acre ridge field when a neighbor came to tell me that my Dad was taken bad. Esther's husband, Charles's father Bill, had gone not all that long before: heart. Cancer took Dad then. There's that bond, too, the shock of the heavy joy of harvest interrupted by death.

Probably, though, it was just as much the ducks that tied me to Christensens' as anything else. Their small farm corners on the reedy end of a spring-fed lake. Walleyes spawned in their creek in those days, and maybe still do. Don Smart, who shared his BB gun with me through my long wait for a first shotgun, finally got old enough to court Charles's sister. After a decent interval he was also invited to hunt mallards — the generic duck in our area — and teal, in that reedy end. I can't count high enough to remember how many pails of water I had to pump for Smart's cow before Don took me along to my first waterfowl opening. The opening itself, however, I've not been allowed to forget.

Nearsighted, equipped with the secondhand experience offered by too many years of barbershop *Field and Stream* reading, I'd never seen a genuine duck up close. In that first early light, the decoys bobbing in a J-shape before Charles's and Don's blind a hundred yards away, I held forever on a hovering blue-winged teal, finally shut both eyes and shot, waded out and picked up — a kingfisher. This shame has never been allowed to fade from the annals of my sporting life; Charles and Don have seen to it that even the double I made on genuine teal later that day didn't wash out the stain of honest stupidity. Now, though I've learned to recognize the high "yike" and half-moon cheek mark of the male bluewing, I

25

still see my buddies' snaggle-toothed grins in nightmares. But this is all prelude.

No matter what my grade point average, I came home from college for the duck opening unless Wisconsin had experienced one of its rare volcanic eruptions; that is, always. One year I arrived at my mother's house with a temperature of 104 and tonsils the size of grapefruit. As Mom needed the car to drive to work, I crawled out of hot, dry sheets at 4 a.m. to walk the three miles to Christensens'. Encased in hippers and hunting jacket, Ithaca in hand, I felt like the lead in a horror movie. I still see Mom's unbelieving look, her face lit by Orion's radiance, as I scuffed off up the road. She didn't even try to dissuade me, just saved her steamy breath.

The hour walk to Charles's was broken only by gallops when I happened upon someone's wakeful German shepherd or rottweiler. When Christensens' house came into view my hunting jacket was soaked with sweat and the fever was clearly broken. The farmhouse, made of those cast cement blocks that are supposed to look like shaped stones, said 1907 on the peak. Charles, looking somewhat younger than that, waited on the back steps, the smell of bacon and flapjacks wafting from the cavernous kitchen behind him. "Good!" he said, "right on time," and led the way to the lane that would bring us to the lake. I had refused his offer of breakfast, not sure it would make it past my still-swollen tonsils. Don, the BB buddy, was passing on the opening because he had finally married Charles's sister. His full-time job delivering fuel oil was the utterly logical result of that rash step.

Along gravely sidehills, past the Brueghel hayfield—long, tilted, edged with scrub oak—through an old, fine family cemetery crackling with frosty milkweed and thistle, and then, finally, on our bellies, humping bags of decoys, we progressed toward the blinds. "Leave the kingfishers alone," said Charles.

I tossed Don's seven falsies, six of Sears' best papier-mâché and an irresistible wooden drake with a movable head, out in front of the blind in a half-moon convoy. Charles, who did his borrowing from city dudes, waded out to sketch a "J" of collapsible rubber "Deeks," the decoy of choice just then. Five minutes after he climbed back into his blind it was opening time.

A morning mist had covered our preparations, but now it cut visibility so drastically that we couldn't identify the big ducks that seemed to be absolutely streaming westward—in range but not, if they turned out to be redheads or pintails, necessarily legal. For all I knew they might have been kingfishers. No shots, then. When the mist cleared, after sunrise, the ducks were gone. Now this was a lovely landscape. Kettle moraine country. Sharply molded gravel ridges. Drumlins. Little farms with lippy roosters and blat-blat-blatting calves. Nowhere the indecency of a noisy milking machine. Serene rurality. But no ducks!

We sat then, in the sun, as trailer trucks began to pound nearby roads, as the first tractors thumped and roared, but these excrescences didn't drown out the whistle of wings, the slight creaking and dividing of feathers, because nothing—nothing—was flying. Through a very long bluebird morning the risen sun cooked us, the decoys, and two yellow-billed coots—mud hens. We looked longingly to the west, to an autumn patchwork hill. At the foot of that hill lay the spring ponds that the lake was named after. Those ponds were posted: "No trespassing—I kin shoot!" by Emmet Haenschke, who dairied there alone. It was more than an even bet that our big ducks had found sanctuary on Emmet's ponds.

Charles's silo pigeons dipped by to keep us company after five hours of landscape beauty. When they flaunted by a third time I swung, fired, and missed the last one—mottled blue and white like a parrot—then saw the duck hawk which had hastened them strike my quarry. Charles yelled: "That big one is a HAWK!" "I'm leaving," I answered.

I gathered in Don's decoys, filled my hippers with muddy east-end water, slouched ashore, decanted muck from the hippers, bagged the decoys and shouldered the Ithaca. Skunked. Again. Reskunked. But Charles ambled over, his slitty Danish eyes always observing me as if I were a corncrib rat or, worse, a page of fine print—anything but a hunter. That's how I felt. Still, he gave me a light right–left to the chest, slipped me a Russet apple (an old tradition with us), and said, "Let's go see if Essie'll part with some home made rye wine for a couple of diseased Nimrods." Charles, a Methodist, knows Nimrod from one of those few Sundays he stayed awake in church. Scripture, of course, comes early in the service. He said "Nim-rod" kind of like "Numb-skull." We went.

Esther, hair covered with a big red handkerchief, was scrubbing eggs. She halted her work to lay out fresh molasses cookies with white frosting, along with two mugs of the rye wine and even two big bowls of pears home-canned with honey. (Esther is a teetotaler, but makes a little wine for the weak and wayward.) The rye wine was grainy, like walnuts or heavy rye bread, and ultimately very warming, but she cut off the supply just when it seemed to promise salvation. Then, poker-faced, she did ask, "Where are the ducks!"

"Yeah," said Charles, "Where *is* the ducks?" This with a smart-assed grin at the grammar-bound college kid.

"Well," and here Esther walked toward the window that framed that orange-beige-yellow hill at the west end of the lake, "I believe you might walk over to Emmet Haenschke's and ask permission to hunt. Emmet used to court Dick's mother." This was news to me. "Dick, you just mention Gert Yatzeck and Emmet's old Model A. If you're not in too much of a hurry Emmet'll give you permission by about three o'clock. He does like to talk, but three's chore time. Then go to his west pasture, kind of sneak through that low, boggy spot toward the spring ponds that feed the lake. I s'pose you might find a mallard or two in there — they've been flying in all morning. If they don't come to you you have to go to them."

"Mom, how do you know so much about Emmet's land?" Charles was usually quicker. "Gert wasn't the only girl Emmet courted," was the answer. "But his land's too boggy."

Emmet was talkative. How was Gert doin', hadn't seen 'er in a coon's age, still workin' at the bank? Didn't get to town much, rheumatism and cows, between 'em, kept him busy. Have a pickle? (Emmet didn't run to cookies.) What's Aunt Margaret up to now Roy's passed away? (He seemed absolutely bent on going through all eleven of my mother's full and half siblings. Esther came in for some attention, too. Altogether positive.) Emmet did go on. But the rank fumes of "Bigger Hair" from a cherrywood pipe, the almost *flavor* of oak in the potbelly, enriched the air and gave substance to his slow elicitation of a world he had left some time before. A bachelor, one of a dying breed, he cared about his former world, remembered it with great fondness. Only thing was, the world that could move him was real, experienced. Emmet knew nothing of Russia or Brazil. (This was before TV enlightened us.) I guess Emmet would have to be called a provincial, a mossback. But he was a hard worker, even as farmers measure, free with his pickles and even his west pasture, to those who cared to get to know him. Only not in a hurry. I miss Emmet.

He walked Charles and me out to the creek, pointed us west toward the spring holes two forties (half a mile) away at the foot of that handsome hill. He'd had to get his cows in anyhow, he and his half-collie Max, and he didn't mind the company. Seemed as though he had seen some ducks dropping in there earlier. "Say hello to Gert, mind! And you, Charles, greet Esther for me!" And I thought, "How is it that Mother never mentioned Emmet?" And I knew, "Because he stayed on the farm; she went to town."

The creek ran noisily over Waukesha County granite, and covered our approach. The bogs were mostly dry. Even the long, slow creep through the cattails went easy. (I can usually get sopping wet in a light dew.) Charles snaked up to the last curtain of green, fine stems, parted them at water level, froze, then snaked back. "Mallards, my Gosh! A hundred anyway. Wind's behind us, so they ought to come right over us when we spook 'em. Or do you college boys groundswat ducks?"

I was doubly nettled. Here was the ghost of that blasted kingfisher again. "Tell you what, Charles." But we were talking too much, though I just had to show some hunting know-how. "I'll work around behind 'em. When I'm opposite, I'll yell and jump 'em. Then they'll come over you sure. You just be careful to shoot high."

"No . . ." But this *was* talking too much. The ducks would move soon anyway to feed in the corn stubble. "I'll creep 'em," said Charles. "You're sort of heavy on your feet."

I am, of course. I've felt fat and nearsighted all my life. But I hunt to escape that image and now I was—well—pissed.

O.K. then, we'll jump 'em right now!" I stood up straight and hurled myself right through that bamboo curtain of cattails, toward the increasingly loud duck talk, with Charles right behind me. "Ker-SPLOOSH!"

The pond was about four feet deep and passing cold. The ducks rose right up before us into the wind, at a forty-five-degree angle, a silver-gray, nut-brown metallic green wave—sort of a mallard tsunami. Charles and I worked our pump guns as if demented. Then we kicked off our hippers and started swimming after greenheads, the birds that had rained back down and were now flapping for shelter in the far reeds.

It was, I guess I said already, numbingly cold. Not all of the ducks were hard hit. Nevertheless—I swim better than I sneak—we caught 'em: two brown hens, four big green-headed, silver-vested drakes. Only two were stone dead in the water. We caught 'em, gathered 'em, retrieved our shotguns from the lone willow trunk at the edge of the pond, and sloshed directly toward Christensens'. Emmet would be in the barn milking now. Cows aren't partial to guests during milking; we could bring over a brace of birds in the morning. When we got to higher ground we did stop to squeeze out our jeans, beat each other warm with our hunting jackets, stuff our wet underwear in our pockets. We had to be quick; evening brought a cold east wind.

Esther took one look at us and started running two hot baths in the laundry tubs. When we'd both gone through, we found bathrobes—Charles's and one of his father Bill's —on chairs in the kitchen, another mound of cookies, and smoking cups of hot, mulled rye wine. With cinnamon. We partook. Before long, even before the wine was gone, Esther came in the back door with six naked mallards and a pot of gizzards and livers. Somehow her competent exertions put us "hunters" to shame a little. It wasn't anything, she said, just the matter-of-fact doing—gutting, picking—and the roasting to come, while we sat warm and naked under the bathrobes. I didn't notice my tonsils at all.

"Emmet sent greetings," said Charles. "Thought he might," said Esther.

August 1995

Forty years have gone since that evening. I've not been guilty of another kingfisher—one was enough. I've never filled up on mallards again, either. But in all that time I can't remember anything tastier than those molasses cookies and hot rye wine. Or anyone more competent and, modestly, triumphant than Esther Christensen.

Too Hasty for Coon

For Mr. and Mrs. Ray Honeyacre

I suppose it must have been October. I'd finished college, had my first teaching job, and was looking for a place, an occasion, to hunt.

My only connection in that neck of the woods was Steve, a former student of mine in Madison, a smart, restless fellow raised on the Wolf River. He planned to have his first million by the time he hit thirty-five, was turning over real estate like a skunk upending rocks for grubs, but could maybe just spare a quick evening for the hounds. He took me along to the Boecks's farm.

Now my friend Steve was restless, even pushy, but Rhiney Boecks, a deer hunting buddy of Steve's dad's, was as hard to push as a hay rope. When we got there it was still light. Steve left the car at a trot; Rhiney had finished chores, but now he was ready for a little talkin' and spittin', and after that, there were the chickens.

Rhiney's chickens seemed to be all over the acreage. A random redbone hound and some rusty chicken wire had led to a poultry breakout, and as we sat spittin', the apple orchard was filling up with Cornish Cross meat chickens going to roost. They had to be gathered safe from the mink before Rhiney would set a dog on track.

We gathered. We climbed apple trees. Rhiney and his boys worked slow and easy, and the chickens hardly stirred in their sleep. Steve and I plucked down nine-pound, squawking, defecating hens and seven-pound roosters, wings beating like barn boards. I groped clumsily and had a couple of ripped thumbs for my trouble. Steve snatched chickens out of the trees 'til Hell wouldn't have it, caught a bloody nose and a fairly purple eye, but got the job done. He must have brought in fifty by himself. "Now let's go!" he said.

"Well," said Rhiney, "the dogs are in the loose box in the barn. We can take a look." Those hounds, two blueticks and the errant redbone, Nancy, Ranter, and Fox, rang like heavy bells at the sight of Rhiney in the evening. In the loose box, which connected with an outside run through a hole cut in the side of the barn, their eyes glowed green and electric. Taut haunches and torn ears spoke of readiness and experience. They looked like chasers.

We didn't look long. Steve threw a sack with climbing irons liberated

31

from the telephone company over his shoulder. One of his schemes was to catch a pair of young coons, breed them, and start a fur farm. Rhiney took a .22 single shot and a lantern out of the mud room. Rhiney's boys, as many as there were dogs, pulled on hip boots and thrust leashes into their pockets. We were ready.

"But, hey, how 'bout some medsun," said Rhiney. "Some o' that u-rine from the sick horse." "Oh, cripes," muttered Steve, reducing his gallop to a trot as we came into the oat field above Boecks's slough. But he pulled a pint of Royal Host out of a pocket—he had come prepared—and Rhiney imbibed. "Now let's move!" said Steve. But we didn't. We stood in the oat stubble on that little hill and we all imbibed, except Steve. He was no teeto-taler, but when he hunted, by criminy, he meant to hunt. I flopped down on some broken straw bales, forgotten in the fury of harvest. Rhiney drawled, "All right, now the pump's primed." And just then Fox said, "H-u-u-u!" and Ranter said, "H-o-o-o!" and the dogs moved like panthers and there was a sliver of moon at most and just a touch of white mist was rising in the low spots. "H-o-o-o!" went Ranter again and "Ha-ha!" went Fox. "Jeepers, that's a nice sound," said Rhiney. He was old enough to say jeepers. He bit off a chew of Brown Mule. "How soon'll they tree?" asked Steve.

The joy of it, the special thrill of running coon with hounds, is that it happens at night, in night's different world. Every tree, every bush is new and strange. You hear more when you see less. You imagine the hounds running lynx, cougar, though an old boar coon is quite able to drown a dog or rip up the hand or leg of an incautious hunter. There is a primal, ancient smoky joy in running coon, but the tempo is set by the coon and the hounds, not by the hunters. This was hard on Steve, who liked to drive fast cars and use two telephones at once. "Can't we cut around and bushwhack the coon?" Steve pleaded, twenty minutes after boys and dogs had run out of hearing. "Can't we speed this process up some?" "Well," said Rhiney, "—pass that medsun will yuh?—when we hear the dogs again we can maybe figger where th' coon is headin', but it's best to sit 'til we hear Nancy tree. Nance trees nice." Steve, who had yet to sit down, fidgeted until his climbing irons clanked. Then, after some while, "Ho-oo-ee!" went what had to be Nancy. Steve was down the hill and going thirty before Rhiney could cap the medsun. "Don't shoot Nance . . ."

"VAROOM! Vroom-vruroom-rawrr!" "What in Hell is that?" "Fox Val-ley Speedway . . . just over t'hill," Rhiney got out, after five minutes of howling, rusty stock car mufflers had thoroughly deafened us. "But how can you hear the dogs, then?" "In between," said Rhiney. "Just in be-tween. I kin hear 'em. I c'ld hear Nance anywhere."

I am making a story of Steve's impatience, but I myself have become restless. I want to take you right to the tree, the coon, the hounds throbbing as if with current in lantern light. I don't even have time "in between," as Rhiney said, to really, truly hear the dogs, or to seek them aurally when they are silent. I am also, now, thirty years further along. Everything, even Christmas, comes, moves, faster.

Rhiney and I sauntered down the hill on Steve's hot track. He was long gone, "gone away" as the English say of a fast fox. Rhiney stumped companionably along under the roar of the race cars, knowing his hounds and land so well that even in the dark, deafened, he had a good idea where the coon had led the dogs. Off ahead of us, across the deep slough that we were circling, Steve was checking all the tree tops for coon eyes with his five-cell light. "Hasty young gaffer," said Rhiney. "Decent, but hasty. Th' dogs are, maybe, two sloughs over."

The racket of the race cars quit, and again the "Ho!" and the "Ha!" of the dogs gladdened the night. Nancy was still barking tree, "Ho-ee!", but apart from her, beyond her singing, Ranter and Fox seemed to be running a different animal. We had just time to hear Steve splash, at speed, into the second slough and toward the treeing Nancy, when the dragsters started up again. Steve's light bobbed crazily across the water and reeds. He wasn't sauntering.

The car roars were louder this time, maybe because we had come out from the shadow of the hill, and I couldn't talk to Rhiney for noise. I could think, though. I swished my pacs through frosty oat stubble and then, then . . . my hand remembers the tiny, quick flame of stinging nettle, the graininess of frost-nipped deer fern, that grew near the slough willow and swamp maple. My hand's memory is sharp. But I remember, too, that my thought, under the nasty clatter, was sad. I remembered running dogs twenty years before that in quieter times. I thought of the loss of eye and ear space to encroaching concrete and motors, of all the horses, Nell and Sal and Linda, dry bones now, replaced by stinking iron. I was, I am, a stupid romantic. I mourn the loss of the old, quiet country, when you could hear the deer fern, as I certainly could not that night.

"Medsun," shouted Rhiney, right in my ear, and I passed him the bottle Steve had forgotten, shared it. The motors stopped, then.

Nancy was treeing just around the bend of the slough, forefeet braced against the broad trunk of an old, squat swamp maple, the kind that's hard to drop and that tries to drop on you. Good. It was all right, the chanting dog, Steve swarming up the tree in his irons to catch the coon alive, and close now, finally honoring Nancy's tree bark, Ranter and Fox closing in, yipping. Coon eyes sparked just above Steve's climbing light. Four eyes. "Two cubs," he sang out. "Just let me get the bag over 'em an' I'll have my brood stock." Enterprise was about to triumph. But Rhiney said, "Hold on, Stevey, here come th' ma!" He'd seen what I, concentrated on Steve's success, almost missed.

A child-sized, silver-tipped black ball rolled just past the lantern Rhiney had lit and set down. Ranter and Fox lunged close behind it. The big ball bounded over a maple root and expanded into a forty-pound sow coon, kind of impatient to retrieve the cubs she'd left in the tree for safekeeping. Steve was on her route. She was up twelve feet of trunk and six feet of Steve before his flashlight hit the ground. She and the cubs splashed into the slough-edge rushes just as Steve, yowling, "Get 'em Nance!", impacted on the hard-trodden cow path. Then Nancy, Ranter, and Fox blasted off over Steve, who was just rising out of the tangle of his climbing irons. Much of his difficulty was caused by the coon sack that had dropped back over his head as the sow coon swarmed him. "Well," said Rhiney as the hounds whooped off after the waterborne coon, "I guess Stevey could use some medsun now . . ." Steve drank. He smoked in the chill air, the slough water boiling off of him, and he drank again, sputtered and coughed and drank.

It was a fair night for coon. We lost those three in the slough, ran two more but never treed, heard a whole symphony of hound music, and thought about Steve and haste. Rhiney was quiet, but his boys, when they came up with us, tended to poke Steve up some, as you poke a damp fire: not too vigorously, but thoroughly. Steve took it well, bagged his climbers and cut his speed. He seemed relieved, though, when the intermittently roaring racers cut the Boecks boys' chaffing. I believe that he'd always seen a lot of sense in technology, even if I couldn't.

About eleven we decided to hang it up and get on back. The dogs, tired from this first run of the year, walked along on loose leashes. We all felt that the main event had already occurred. We dawdled around the slough, up the hill, and past the straw pile. We scuffed along, Rhiney's boys walking the dogs ahead. The lantern lit the whitish undersides of the apple leaves, and the winding down of the racers just let us catch, for what seemed the hundredth time, an imitation of Steve's desperate, "Get 'em Nance!" as he flew from the maple. Then it happened.

It's really not believable. But try, anyway. Nancy picked up her ears, put down her nose, "ho"ed, and broke for the hen house. Fox and Ranter took off, too, through the rusty yard wire, through the square chicken trapdoor that we'd forgotten to bolt. All three hounds, bellering like sixty, disappeared into the looming hen house. Then a hundred Cornish Cross chickens began to sail through the rusty mesh windows, big, white chickens in full chicken flight, and after them a good-sized mutant coon, fire-red in the lantern light and covered with feathers, and then the baying of the dogs, too close to the ground to make it out the high windows but not about to be forgotten. Of course, I haven't forgotten them.

Steve stayed to help put those hundred chickens away again. Rhiney's boys rolled laughing out of the apple trees that the chickens tried, again, to roost in. Rhiney and I finished the medsun nailing new mesh on the chicken house windows. The hounds, returned after a fruitless, joyful hour pursuing that red coon, quietly stowed away the hot mash and kibble mixture that Rhiney kept them on. After midnight, the racers were still. We drove on home. And now, three decades later, I've lost track of Steve, "decent, but hasty." Rhiney's under the wild chicory; his boys are gone too — one to 'Nam, two to the city. A superhighway has flattened the little oatfield hill and filled in the sloughs. But I can still hear, as Rhiney said, "in between," Nancy's "ho-oo-ee!"

1992; revised 1995

My Yatzeck aunts kept a red-brown biter of mailmen named Gus. A Scottish terrier named Tuffy hunted crayfish and smelled of lake at Okauchee. You've met Irish Jukes. I like them for their patience with us, their teaching through example, not words. The coon hounds, though, bewitch with gaunt, leopard quickness, leather endurance, and trail music. Bugle Ann, the name of a hound in a book, is the name of all real hounds. They almost balance the ugly clamor and clumsy haste of the "real" world.

Mother's Day Opening

There was a time when walleye season in Wisconsin opened on Mother's Day weekend. Political correctness has since changed the fishing calendar, but I will speak here of that earlier time, and not without nostalgia. It used to be possible, even likely, to satisfy both the mothers and the commercial interests of America with a gift of fish. Alas, I speak of times long gone.

My colleague Mike has a Ph.D. in Russian history, a beautiful wife, and two promising sons. At that time, though, he possessed what was more than all these: He owned a Rhinelander guide boat. Wood strakes, sharp keel, lovely curving gunwales, you could—well, I couldn't, but he could—row this handmade beauty with one oar while trolling the reefs on Big Muskellunge Lake. The guide boat stayed on course. Since it was made of fir it tended to leak and rot unless constantly sanded, painted, even, ultimately, fiber-glassed one evil day. That boat put pressure upon both family and academic life, but Mike's fishing buddies loved him for it.

Mike and I then, on a few—too few, in retrospect—of those Mother's Day openings, would lug his marvelous light boat to Big Muskellunge, Little St. Germain, and Helen Lake, all near the fleshpots of Woodruff. We carried muskie tackle but generally fished for walleyes. We took a tent, camp stove, sleeping bags, and rain gear—in short, we moved our essential households north for a retreat every early May. "Retreat" because this was, really, a religious experience, fraught with time-tested ritual.

For instance, forty days before opening was the proper time to sharpen hooks, lay in new line, watch and pray over lake maps, that is, properly observe the fisherman's Lent, the period between losing the pickup through the last of the ice on Lake Winnebago and initiating the new Jeep by driving north for walleyes. We religiously stopped for chili (with pasta instead of beans) at the A&W in Antigo. By four we were stocking up on bacon, eggs, and butter in Woodruff (we'd brought our own potatoes and onions) and deciding, after no debate, on T-bones and Jim Beam for dinner at the campsite. Then we perused three-inch shiner minnows, choosing only alpha males. These liturgical offices accomplished, we made our pilgrimage back east to the white sand of the campground on Big Muskellunge Lake.

We set up camp only after a good long breath of lake and conifer air. The fire, for cooking but more for atmosphere, was made with driftwood gathered on the lake shore but had to include those lichen-rich dead fir branches that provide northern incense, the sweet spirit of spring fishing. No hallucinatory drug is as destructive of civilized preconceptions. That lichen aroma turns any nerd into Paul Bunyan. Ground sheet, tent, sleeping bags are secondary. You can lean against that lichen incense and dream. Of what?

Of walleyes. Of monster muskies guzzling your innocent walleye bait. Of that, say, eight-pound white-eyed *Stizostedion vetreum*, dorsal fin raised in spiky defiance, that will ennoble the blank spot above your mantel (a dollar an inch in those days, though we never quite needed a taxidermist). After these visions it was time for a seminar on present fishing conditions.

At what temperature do walleyes spawn and would they be ready to feed tomorrow? In which of the local lakes might spring warming be furthest along? Should we choose little Helen or St. Germain? Ought we rather try muskie fishing? When the Jim Beam made our talk wander, it was time to cover the fire with sand, stash the cooler with the butter and bacon in the station wagon so the raccoons wouldn't trash breakfast, and maybe spend a fine minute tracing the moon's path on Big Muskellunge before turning in.

And up at five. If we'd decided for muskies, we'd just slide that Rhinelander right into the lake before us. Said Big Muskellunge, Mike claimed, held no northerns, so if you got a strike you were into a tiger. When I caught an eleven-pound northern there once, he simply refused to recognize it as a fish. "Where'd you snag that rotten cedar post?" he snarled. I was almost convinced that I'd have to hurl my fish in the campfire. Such was, and is, the force of Mike's piscatorial authority.

Usually, though, we would start at Little St. Germain, shallow enough to offer early warming and a chance at a nice mess of 'eyes. By 7 a.m., then, eggs and bacon digesting nicely, we'd be pitching shiners on no. 8 hooks, two feet down from heavy split shot sinkers, at the barely greening weed beds on the reefs. Cast and super-slow retrieve, stop and start, ease the shiners across the beds, drop them over the edge into deeper water while fastened with two anchors to keep parallel to our target zone, wait for the two-inch, almost imperceptible dip of the rod. I can feel it in my fingers any time I choose. I can imagine it much more easily than I can convince spring walleyes to bite. In May there doesn't seem to be anything that needs doing quite so achingly.

Anyway, there came a spring opening when morning and afternoon— 7 to 5—spent this lovely way led to grinding, grim frustration. Mike, careful and wily contender that he is, had religiously switched reefs, weed beds, speed of retrieve, baits, angles of approach, all day. Mike generally catches fish when I don't, because he works at it seriously, thinks himself into the walleye's situation. I've known him to spot two passing fish, choose a jig—red—and tie it on, cast twice and bring in both fish. I sit in the stern (I'd upend us if I sat in the bow) and I cast all right, but it doesn't occur to me to vary bait, presentation, or location; I tend to be watching an osprey's nest in that tall white pine, or brooding about Genghis Johnson, the sadistic dean of our small college. I love to fish but I don't take the trouble to learn how.

To this habitual contradiction between Mike's craft and my lack of cunning St. Germain decided to add an utter injustice. On the second cast of the day, while I was undoing a backlash, the rod dipped slightly. Feeling the slightest of hindrances I hauled back instantaneously and dramatically—though I often lose my fish through this lack of patience. Against all science and expectation I became aware of a lively and serious weight on my line. Walleyes don't fight hard, but this nice three-pounder gave me a fair struggle. We don't see three-pounders often, do we? And Mike said, "This will be a day, no?"

No. Where Mike's finesse ought to have filled the boat, St. Germain quit on us. Mike exerted every wile, experimented with every depth, spinner, and jig, and came up skunked. It was a wretchedly unfair opening. When we scraped in on the landing, cranked that beautifully restored boat onto the trailer and headed back to the tent where the Jim Beam was waiting, we had only that single, unlikely, now rather stiff three-pound walleye. I was seriously embarrassed.

What do you do? Mike had, of course, maintained his manners, been correct, had even yelled, "Way to go!" as he netted the fish. But that walleye had hung around us all day, alone on a heavy stringer, hindering the one-handed control of the Rhinelander boat. By 5 p.m. Mike's sunny nature was a tad overcast. He tended to respond to my quiet remarks on herring gulls, or on the insignificance of actually *catching* fish, with sibilant monosyllables ending in explosive "t's." I wasn't at all sure that the lichen incense would work its usual magic that evening. I felt the need to reach a serious decision about the one fish. "Let's eat the oversized sucker," I offered. "We don't have to ice 'im. We can maybe take tomorrow morning's fish home with us. I've been wanting to try onion-stuffed walleye anyway, this one's almost big enough." "Done!" said Mike, half-grim, half-relieved. For a Russian historian he has an unusually personal hatred of rank injustice. This walleye was *wrong.*

So I scaled, Mike chopped onions, and we buried the pike surrounded by potatoes under a really fine driftwood and fir fire, let the fir burn down to glowing embers, and meanwhile dropped the Jim Beam level considerably while waiting for pike and spuds to get succulent. When injustice had been reduced to an onion-pungent rack of bones, Mike's spirits visibly rebounded. He offered a toast, "To your fish! May you catch a six-pounder tomorrow." We drank to that, though I crossed my fingers behind my back. I wanted *two* six-pounders tomorrow, one for each of us.

Just then, out of the reddening corner of my eye, I caught motion in the fire's far penumbra. This movement, though it was quick, seemed black and white. I decided to ignore it. I even toasted Mike back: "May no one be skunked tomorrow!" Mike clinked glasses, though somewhat thoughtfully. He'd caught that movement at the rim of the firelight too. "We might just get skunked yet tonight," he muttered. "I think our cooking has attracted a guest." I saw, this time, quite clearly, the tall black and white plume as it passed between the two young firs. "Scat," I hissed.

For a time this seemed to work. When the blue enamel pot boiled we poured after-dinner coffee, the grounds settled with the morning's eggshells. Coffee royale seemed a likely idea. So we poured the remains of the Jim Beam bottle into generous camping mugs with the coffee and happily offered more toasts. Not much later, we began to see skunks left and right. We rose and backed toward the tent. After some tense time a *mosaic* of skunks rather like an Escher engraving — or as if seen through the eyes of a bee — approached a mosaic of blue coffee pots and seized a veritable Sierra of walleye skeletons. After that we were disturbed no more. And this was rather unsurprising, as we found ourselves within the tent and behind the double zipper. Even more amazingly, there was no odor at all, just lichen incense.

The next morning we pitched out of a tent that neither of us remembers entering. We reheated the remains of the coffee on the Coleman, didn't even attempt a campfire, put eggs and bacon out of our minds just in time to avoid nausea. We broke camp without much discussion, thought we might try Helen Lake on the way home, resolved not to give St. Germain another shot at us.

The smaller Helen, once Mike had most precisely backed the Rhinelander down the narrow, stony landing, was lovely to us. The shiner minnows that we had acquired on the way plopped neatly against the steepest bank. The fifteen-inch walleyes made the monofilament veritably hum through the for once really sky blue water. In two hours — plenty of time to arrive home with summer light and honor — we had two handsome limits of pan-sized filets.

We bought roses on the way home, but there was, for once, no need to buy pizza to replace missing walleyes. The mothers and children seemed properly impressed, smiled more than widely. There was no need for the ritual question: "Where are the fish?" We dined scrumptiously. And, next morning before work, Mike caught me absentmindedly gathering sticks, looking for lichen, in front of our college's Main Hall.

August 1995

The opening of walleye season quite unreasonably bulks as large in the sportsman's year as Christmas in normal folks' calendar. These days, green or almost autumnal brown packages of surprise, vary life's sustaining but predictable pale gray. I suppose that Mother's Day might have a similar cachet for mothers, though I rather doubt it.

First Goose

When I was young, my hunting range was the section of rocky pasture, stubble field, brushy fence line, and untillable marsh that I could reach on foot from the back door of a farmhouse in Genesee village. I saw geese, dreamed of geese, but never got near them. I have still in my memory a calendar picture of a hunter on a snowy hill. He is dressed like an Orvis gent, has a Canada goose by the neck in his left hand and a Browning over-under in his right. He is watching the smoke curl from the chimney of *his* farmhouse. Though I never knew a farmer, then, whose artillery came from anywhere but Montgomery Ward or who hunted in anything but bib overalls, that dream of solid success and triumphal homecoming haunted me for forty years. Hunters, generally, dream of the concrete rewards of goose necks and venison haunches. It took me twenty-five years to grasp my first goose neck.

I had, of course, gotten the occasional chance at a low flock, usually a flock of six or eight, on the first day of duck season or while stomping a marsh for a native pheasant in late October. Canadas always look as big as Zeppelins, and as slow, but my surprised snap shots never got me more than the shiver of awe that seeing the big birds always evokes. So, I decided, like everyone else, that Horicon was the place to go to shoot a Canada, although I dislike, on principle, driving anywhere to hunt. Game ought to come from the land that you live on and know: hunters like me are atavistic; we live quite happily in a long-gone past.

But the land I lived on then was a fifty- by one-hundred-foot lot in Appleton. The game was an occasional fat and cheeky gray squirrel, and shooting in town was not encouraged. So, I mounted a one-man expedition to Horicon, to a shooting camp run by Ray Schultz, who spent his summers selling shiners and renting leaky boats on Winnebago, where his house was, but who lived during the goose season in a rusty trailer on a forty outside of Horicon, renting out goose blinds and despising bad shots. I think *the* pleasure of the season, for him, was the regularly repeated realization that most hunters could not knock down a Canada as deftly as he could, at seventy-three.

Anyway, I drove early one morning down to Ray's camp. There I was led in the drizzly dawn, by one of the cronies who gathered there, to a blind

41

behind a fallen oak. I watched lots of geese go by. They came and left at every height and by every point of the compass. Ray and his brother coots had each killed a goose by 8:15. I, armed with my first, used Browning—traded up to through fifteen years of skimping on underwear—swung, led, and snap shot at exactly twenty-five geese. I know this because I fired both barrels each time until I had only one shell left (I missed with it, too). I'd brought one box of twos, and Ray sold me another, grimly and at a high price. At noon he refused to sell me a second box at any price, called me, quietly, painful names, and sent me away with the hot Browning in my right hand and no goose neck in my left. Skunked!

There were other expeditions, not essentially different. The steady but apparently unhurried flight of lines and "vees" of balloon-like Canadas crossed my sights, invaded my dreams, and blighted my self-confidence all that fall. Finally, I invited Mike, walleye fisher and skunk watcher, whose aim and experience were, I thought, enough inferior to mine to give *me* a few of the laughs and giggles that I had provided for the coots during that autumn's disasters. I chose badly.

This time we drove Mike's Chevy, weighed down with twos and guns and us, to a public hunting area. As the sun began to break the horizon, we took our place in the Maginot line, in a field of red willow and Reed's canary grass. Before the geese had fully achieved take-off, half a mile away and beyond the refuge line, the field erupted with gunfire. Gracefully, disdainfully, the Canadas floated up to an altitude of two hundred yards and passed over. No geese fell, of course. We didn't shoot. Hell, we felt more like taking cover, and by nine o'clock most of the other sports were out of shells, thirsty, or both. Anyway, the crowd thinned—the geese seemed to have quit flying for the morning—and Mike and I were left in the willow and tall grass. We drank our coffee, ate liverwurst, and let our ears clear of concussion. Then we spread fifty yards apart to await a possible tardy flight.

One came. A ruler-straight line of nine or ten geese driving right over Mike. He spit out his liverwurst, inclined his long Model 12, swung until the barrel was vertical, and slapped the trigger. A goose spiraled down. Mike ran the hundred yards or so to the point of impact and returned with the flapping prey, goose neck firmly clutched in right hand, Winchester in left. (Mike's a lefty.) No hill, no farmhouse, but a palpable success, nevertheless.

"How in hell did you do that?" I anguished. My expertise was in *missing* geese. I really wanted to know. "Just swing and slap," said Mike. My feelings were mixed. I congratulated him, the hunting buddy I had picked for his inexperience, but my eyes were bright green.

We waited until noon for another low flight, hit Horicon for a burger and beer, and then Mike decided, since I was too grumpy to decide anything, that we ought to rent a blind from a local farmer for the afternoon and try our luck—my luck, since he had filled up—right in among the cornfields. I agreed. It seemed hopeless, but I couldn't resist. It is *such* a crummy feeling to be a bad sport *and* a bad shot.

Orville Tanner's blinds were set, properly distanced from each other, on a corn stubble hill that sloped east toward the marsh. This field was backed on the west by at least a section of uncut, goose-ridden corn. The blinds cost five bucks apiece, and, said Orville, we could return free as often as we liked until I got my goose. Like Ray Schultz, Orville could size up a hunter.

That afternoon—as the geese returned to the refuge—began kind of like the morning I had spent at Ray Schultz's goose camp. I wiped out my shells, and then we divided Mike's. I blew away that dozen, and we split the remaining twelve. As we did this I realized—clearly—that Mike had fired just one shot on his first goose hunt and that there was one large gray-black-and-white bird in the back of his Chevy. I, on the other hand, had shot up, in the course of a single late afternoon, thirty-seven twelve-gauge magnum loads. Mike was no Ray Schultz. He was quiet and concerned, sportsmanlike, and absolutely in control of his triumph. He was at once relaxed and intent on spotting new flights of Canadas for me. If his two sons hadn't been rather young to be orphaned, I would have tried a shot at him, but I'm convinced that I would have missed.

Ultimately, another group of eight geese slid toward the blind, Indian file and forty yards up. Anxiously, I watched them come. They seemed to be braking a little, getting ready to settle into the refuge, three fences east. They seemed even slower than the Goodyear blimp, more like the spiders that float by on a length of web and a light wind in an October duck marsh. When the leader was a yard from perpendicular to me, I swung up, slapped the trigger, then slapped it again for good measure. The sixth goose in the line set its wings. A hit—or a heart attack from overeating. I wasn't sure which.

I began running down the hill, taking half of the blind with me and barely acknowledging Mike's "Good show!" The goose made a perfect landing and hunkered down thirty yards beyond the first fence. As I crossed the fence, Browning at the ready, the Canada began to run. I drew a bead on his head, thirty yards away, and discovered that I had not reloaded. Miraculously managing not to drop the shells, I ejected the smoking empties and slid in fresh twos. The Canada, now at fifty yards, was hitting his stride. Blam, blam! No effect, except that he hopped the second fence with more rear-end English than he had been using.

At the second fence, having gained back the twenty yards and again managing to reload, I shot again. The only effect was to knock the goose from his direct escape route and send him at a long angle toward the last fence, the fence of the game refuge itself. As I puffingly vaulted the second fence, I realized three things: (1) that I was out of shells, (2) that my Orvis camouflage parka was neatly pinned by all three strands of barbed wire, and (3) that as a result of this, my head and shoulders, the only unpinned part of me, were about to make sharp contact with a slimy square yard of mud and corn stubble. The ripping of the parka and the splash-crackle of me catapulting into raw Wisconsin were quickly followed by my whining roar to Mike: "Out of shells!" I looked back. My buddy was rolling on the ground in front of what was left of the blind, grasping his lean belly, either poisoned or laughing. I could guess which.

Then I charged, rags of Orvis flying, Browning in both hands as if tipped with a bayonet. The Canada had slowed, but he put on a burst toward that last fence when I was within twenty feet of him. Cradling the gun, I hurled *me*. His neck dropped as I landed with one knee on each of his wings. He didn't stir again.

Not looking at Mike, I lit a Camel, smoked it down to a tiny butt, and field stripped and ground it into the mud, still sitting on the goose. After a while I got up and wandered, quietly, back over the fences and up the hill to Mike, goose neck in my left hand, the scratched and muddy Browning in my right, my Orvis parka flapping like a live, half-plucked vulture. My buddy had recovered his habitual relaxed attitude. Generously repressing a further guffaw, he choked out, "You got 'im."

"Yah," I said, "but I aimed at the leader and the sixth goose came down. How far did you lead *yours* this morning?"

"Hell," said Mike, who rarely curses. "I must have led one goose-length less than you did. I swung on the daddy goose and got the seventh one in line."

Then we went back to the Chevy and drove home to pluck our first Canadas.

October 1984

In April, seen from this attic, the smoke-thin curling threads of north-rowing Canadas mean order, eternal return. The geese hoot like hounds, make speed without apparent haste, measure the flow of the years with unerring accuracy. I have seen them do genuine barrel-rolls returning to the twenty acres of cattails and ditches that is their biannual motel here. They make a lovely old clock, the only timepiece, really.

Thrum-Whoosh

"There are two kinds of hunting: ordinary hunting and ruffed-grouse hunting." Aldo Leopold said that. Maybe he meant that usually one *sees* other kinds of game — a pheasant cock over a marsh edge, with time to wait for the cackle, a rabbit twisting across corn stubble — though it is not unusual to miss them. But a partridge calls attention to himself with the hum of a plucked hay rope and the thrashing of a farm goose dropped down a chimney. If you see him at all through the branches of the white spruce that tiptoes just ahead of every partridge hunter he resembles a pale gray or rusty hardball off a fast bat. Admiration — and low cursing — take up much of the time spent partridge hunting. For an ecologist like Leopold the ruffed grouse must have seemed classic in his ability to demonstrate that man is not the master of nature. "Thrum-whoosh!" "Dammit!"

Raised in open dairy country hunting rabbits and an occasional pheasant, I was years ago surprised to see three brown banty chickens run past me in a new covert near the Wisconsin River. Then "thrum-whoosh" and the banties evaporated. That evening the Currier and Ives calendar on the wall in my dorm room showed me that what I had seen were ruffed grouse. Currier said, quite distinctly, "Dummy!" That's much nicer than what I usually call myself while hunting partridge. Last January, for instance . . .

Last January, Mike, the genuine goose hunter, accompanied me to the Mack Public Hunting Area in Outagamie County to celebrate the last day of the season. Unready for suicide, he had decided to take up partridge hunting. Our outfit included no dog, my L. C. Smith, Mike's uncle's rickety Mossberg bolt, and my know-how. We could have been in a lot better shape.

There is an inch of snow in the Mack this day. The wind fairly sharp in the northwest. The leaves, which excuse misses on grouse in the fall, are all but gone. The silver gray of prickly ash is lightened only here and there by the bright tan beech leaves that always seem to last the winter. The sky is sort of pig-iron gray. Not the best of omens, really.

Lacking dogs, we do our own driving. We walk kind of parallel and fifty yards apart; out of sight of each other in that head-high thicket but still within hearing. After a while we find those tracks: half the size of pheasant tracks, not as narrow as those of a crow, the little snowshoe hairs showing sharply in the fresh snow. In a bit Mike calls urgently, "Do they look like midget chickens?" Remembering Currier, I let him know that they do. Mike has come across a pod of running partridges which, barely recognized, now become three, five, ultimately nine theoretical flight lines sketched by quick red or gray blurs against and then behind prickly ash and alder clumps. The Mossberg burps, catches, burps again. As two buzzing shadows pass me I accomplish a negative double: no birds for two shots at two birds simultaneously in the air. My it's quiet once they're gone!

Limping along on my experience we set about following up. A grouse on the first rise generally flies fifty yards or so. Our blurs don't seem to be able to measure distance, but after busting tag alder and wild grape — which have replaced the beech and prickly ash — for maybe a quarter-mile, we do begin to find wing prints and tracks. The wind has freshened and the birds seem to be running. Mike and I, agreeing to meet at noon on the railroad embankment a mile or so northwest of us, go off in different directions after different birds. We hear partridge flushing. Once, straddling a birch blowdown with my mouth full of wild grapes, I see a gray bird rise and depart *silently*, unhurriedly, in a direction quite beyond the swing of my vine-obstructed Smith. So the buggers don't *have* to "thrum-whoosh" after all! In cover that's a little more open we cut numerous portholes with ounces of eights at further members of the pod but we are unable by noon to bring a single bird to bag.

Of course we discover the mutuality of our failure when we meet, a bit after noon, for the traditional sardine and liverwurst lunch. There's no good excuse not to have a couple of birds by now, but there *are* reasons. Since these reasons — our failure to continue the swing while shooting, my tendency to blow both barrels before the bird is twenty yards away — are really absences of hunting skills, they don't bear discussion. Lunch is quiet, too, like that moment after the grouse departs untouched, only longer.

As we pack up sausage casings and sardine cans Frank Jolin comes along the tracks, that rotten, nasty, superb grouse shot. He has four birds, besides two bunnies, and is thinking of hanging it up for the day. When the ESP of our glum looks enlightens even *him* about our luck, he hands each of us a cottontail. "Go ahead, take 'em, druther eat partridge anyway," and goes off whistling. Yeah, well . . .

Over noon the wind moved right around into the southeast and quieted a bit. Our tracking and blasting has carried us further north in the Mack than we usually go. We decide to keep the wind in our faces and hunt back toward the now quite distant parking lot, the cover where we first ran into the partridge. Twenty-five yards apart this time, hoping that our united firepower may be more effective, we start back.

Afternoons are short in January, the pig iron of the sky darkens rapidly. On this trek back to the car the only signs of life seem to be an occasional dark green cedar or tamarack and, once, the early "hu-*hu*-hu-*huuu*" of a hunting owl. Then, gradually, we begin to collect partridge tracks. They're heading southeast too. We get no more chances to make asses of ourselves over gray or red smudges in the brush, but I do find, maybe half a mile from the parking lot, the heavier wing prints of our rival, the owl, and a couple of black-barred tail feathers. There is *one* hunter in the woods, even with Jolin gone home.

As closing time approaches Mike and I seem to be following what becomes almost a partridge *trail:* three, five, then seven separate tracks converging toward the tamarack woods which shows behind the now imminent parking lot. Given our marksmanship, I suppose we are lucky that the birds don't turn to trample us. Fifteen minutes before sundown we break out of the prickly ash at Mike's Chevy. The grouse tracks have all, by now, ended with wing prints in the snow. The birds have gone to roost.

As Mike opens the tailgate of the Chevy wagon to get the gun cases the late afternoon sun shines out under the lid of cloud in the west. A single old snowdrift powdered with the newer snow juts brightly beneath the tamaracks fifty yards across the lot. Now during the long, fallow return hunt, embittered as it was by the weight of Jolin's rabbits in our jacket pockets, Mike and I had finally found it possible to discuss our errors. I had decided that I need to say something long, like the 23rd Psalm, before swinging on a flushed partridge. Mike, always more practical, felt that *his* problems might lie with the really rickety Mossberg's pattern, or in the load chosen. Spotting the fine layer of new snow on the old drift, he decides to test both possibilities here and now. Replacing the ounce of 8's with a heavy load of 6's, he closes the bolt, levels the piece, and fires. Here a lot of stuff comes down on us all at once.

Ka-BLAM! Thrum-whoosh! Plock! Clank!

"TheLordismyshepherdIshallnot . . ." A neat three-foot pattern appears in the snowdrift. The first partridge departs from the left-hand tamarack. As Mike cranks mightily at the bolt to eject the shell casing (plock!) the Mossberg disintegrates into stock, bolt, and action (clank!). A second partridge sends me back to "TheLord . . ." Mike throws the Mossberg's stock after the third bird. I, abandoning Biblical scholarship, void the Smith at the fourth and fifth. The sharp, dropping, then rising, brazen flash of the sixth and seventh birds in the lurid sunset ends the day, and the lesson. Then, as happens in January at dusk, it got very dark. Mike, or I, might have said something shocking and smelly.

And then . . . well, then February came with a thaw, March with a haze of green on the willows and, as usual, hunting season, looking forward *or* backward, began to show less iron gray, more red golden. We can make out every feather of those last two birds against that crimson sunset. Even the jagged but regular lines of their tufted heads. Mike is talking about a new Ithaca double, open bore. I'm in love with a springer spaniel pup. Leopold was, no doubt, right about the impossibility of mastering nature. But dammit, we'll try again come fall.

December 1987

Every year the antlers of Charles's deer are garlanded, one feather at a time, with gray or red souvenirs of that season's ruffed grouse. They are not, I hope, mere trophies. I see them rather as reminders of Dutch blue October days and of the beauty of the quarry. The sparseness of this collection testifies to the wit of the bird, the dimness of the hunter.

Cause and Effect

The buck stood, steaming blackly, fifty feet south. The point of woods, tall canary grass, aspen, red partridge berries, framed the animal as it stood in the snow. Six years — lives? — waiting for this day, looking now at his first buck over the barrel of the single twenty.

We, Pete and I, had driven those woods west. We walked opposite sides of the ridge, came down into boggy, grassy snow ground, saw one tea-cup-sized track. Stopped to talk at the point of trees, forgetting that print, when the heavy six-pointer broke north, then back east, out of the grass and aspen. Caught out, wet and panting, I voided the whole magazine after, over, under him. Out of sight, into low popple, he came to a stop where Alex saw him.

"Gone," I thought, "*another* miss." Pete, the hunter, swung to intercept if he came back into the point.

Alex told his dad (Mike of the geese and partridge), "He stopped right there, there. I would have shot, but Dick and Pete were in those woods. He just stood. Boy, I wanted to shoot."

Mike is an historian. Lust, then war. Hunger, then revolution. Cause and effect. He'd had Alex carry that twenty empty the whole last season; so he'd remember it's the empty gun that kills men, would learn safety before he *could* shoot. Alex, hungry as only a boy can be hungry for a first buck, had *not* shot, had thought to spare our miserable hides. Had seen that reeking bison, hairy mammoth, and let him go. Rightly. Cause and effect. It wasn't easy, though.

We saw that buck, hooves up, back at the east end of the point. A father/son team had downed him, gutted him, were warm with triumph. But not as warmly proud as Mike was, for Alex hadn't shot. I hope Alex was proud too. Still I know he sees that buck in dreams, hooves up in the shallow snow. Standing framed by partridge berries. Big as life.

October 1993

50

These last four tales have included Mike, professor of Russian history, outdoorsman, and, here, father. In this piece educational and outdoor feats are one. Mike is also a famous outdoor chef. It was his habit to carry salt, pepper, and an onion along the edges, thinking to cook the quarry at the scene of the crime. Once, having hijacked a slow snowshoe hare, we gutted, skinned, spiced, and onioned the big bunny and impaled it upon a hazel spit. We turned it and we waited and we endured the dark looks of another pair of hunters who suspected us of shooting a cottontail out of season. Snowshoes are always in season—and toward sunset we discovered a good reason for this. In the absence of a pressure cooker, their merely barbecued flesh is indistinguishable from boot leather.

Blow in Her Ear

In the 1940s, in my home town, if you were twelve you were old enough to hunt. The cow dog would double as a flushing dog. The gun was whatever stood behind the kitchen door. I hunted for three years with my pal Don, from up the road, before we shot our first rabbit with a single-shot, octagon-barreled, rolling-block-action .22. (We'd run out of shells for our .410s.) It seems to me that we shot it sitting. Our neighbor, Mrs. Barr—who had a parrot and a roomful of canaries—must have liked boys, because she showed us how to clean the rabbit. The plan to supply both our families with winter meat in those days of rationing, hatched at the sight of that enormous cottontail, somehow never worked out.

Where I lived isn't mountain country, but we always hunted toward, and in sight of, "the bluffs," five sixty-foot hillocks that were our western horizon. To me those hills seemed to be the edge of the world. We stayed off the Honeyacres' land, which lay southwest of the bluffs, because Ray Honeyacre was rumored to be a grumpy codger who didn't like boys with guns. What he would do if he ever caught one on his place was unclear, but still utterly terrifying. We stayed off, especially since the Honeyacres' line divided Bloom's from a low, wet piece dotted with quicksand pockets.

We moved away to town, I went to high school and college, hunted less frequently, got married, got a job teaching, got a divorce, and found myself one October at loose ends in life, again hunting toward the bluffs with my Uncle Danny's hammer double and my cousin's dog Peggy.

My cousin, Jim, who had sensibly stayed home in the country, had once hunted with me. I remember making him skin his two first squirrels while I tediously explained the criminality of not cleaning your own game (I had forgotten about Mrs. Barr and that first cottontail). While I was in school, Jim had gotten a job, had married, built a house in our home town, and hunted. Quite broad-mindedly he was allowing a shiftless and divorced professor to borrow his seventy-pound Chesapeake and his father's old double for an afternoon of pheasant hunting.

By 1970 there weren't a lot of pheasants left around that neck of the woods; there weren't even many dairy farms. They were being replaced by subdivisions. The bluffs were still there, though. It was late October and Peggy, by now an old dog, was ready to go. As she and I left Jim's place in

52

my VW, which seemed to shrink as she climbed in, Jim shouted, "Blow in her ear if she won't drop the bird!" I looked at him, at Peggy, and decided not to worry about that problem unless I had to.

Peggy and I began by hunting into a breeze from the west and down the slope of Bloom's south cornfield. The slope and field ended in the blackberry and red willow tangle of a small creek, a jungle that belted the bluffs. The tan stubble produced a covey of Hungarian partridges, but they were leery as cats and jumped twenty yards ahead of me. By the time I had the half-moon hammers cocked, the Hunkies had disappeared against the red-gold haze of the bluffs. Peggy gave me a side glance and kept on hunting. She was clearly no longer in her prime, but she hadn't hunted for a while. She was willing, for now, to put up with the meathead she had begun to suspect I was.

Peggy had always been a straight bird dog. When she got there, she quartered the willows and berry tangles of the creek edge like a field-trial champion—old, maybe, but she knew her trade. When her heavy tail, which could clout like a baseball bat, began to thrash the berry tangle, I got ready. I put my thumbs on the hammers of the old double, rested the butt on my belt buckle, and prayed. There—Peggy lunged into a break in the creekside bushes; there—"cuck-cuck-cuck," a cock bird rose straight up out of the jungle; and *there*—I fired both barrels at once, from the waist, and sat down quite suddenly. The rooster sailed off south. Peggy didn't even look at me this time.

But she gave me one more chance. She had, as I said, always been a straight bird dog (occasionally she might chase a cottontail out of her own backyard), but she must have thought I needed an easier target. After we'd both crossed the creek, at the far edge of the red willow brush, she barked once—like the snort of a diesel tractor starting—and pushed out a bunny that zigzagged up the thirty-degree incline of the bluff ahead of us. She didn't pursue it, just barked in case I was interested. This time I got the double cocked, shouldered, and swinging, let off one barrel at a time, and missed two zags as the cottontail reversed to zigs. Peggy left me.

The cornfield, the creek brush, and three consecutive snafus all drove me to a state of contemplation. After climbing the bluff, I sat down under a scrub oak to wait for Peggy. From there I could see the road where I'd parked the car. I could also see the cornfield, the creek, and the Honeyacres' quicksand bottom where the rooster had disappeared. I drank cider, ate a liver sausage and Gorgonzola sandwich, and thought. I thought about rabbit hunting here years ago with Don and a beagle, and the discovery that cottontails really *do* run in circles, and I thought about the long city years since I'd been here. Then, more and more, I thought about Peggy. Where had she gone? I might be forgiven for missing one of the now rare pheasants, but I wouldn't dare show up at Jim's without his dog. Then I caught sight of her.

She was at the foot of the bluff, to my right and down, over on the Honeyacres' land. At least half of her — thirty-five pounds of her — was visible. Her front half was out of sight in a tumble of fine sand and gravel. She was digging something out of what used to be a warren of skunk dens.

Skunk dens?

"No, no, no!" rolled out ahead of me even before I began to run.

I heard a high "yipe!" saw her lunge deeper, and glimpsed black-and-white fur even before I was close enough for the smell to hit me. She'd killed the skunk which had bitten her. At her age, apparently, she didn't have time to wait until I shot something. Now, followed by me bellowing, she took off straight across the Honeyacres' springhole land, gripping the dead skunk firmly in her mouth, not about to drop it. I thought of rabies, rabies shots, skunk scent, and tomato juice. Jim's last words hit me: "Blow in her ear if she won't drop the bird." If I didn't want to take that skunk to the vet, I'd have to catch Peggy and blow in her ear.

My hot pursuit cooled quickly. I sailed over the first soft spot, came down in a beautiful clump of watercress, and slid under it through sandy black ooze until I was standing on hardpan, up to my armpits in slush. There was nothing to catch hold of, no willow clump nearby and it sure felt like quicksand. I had stopped sinking, but I couldn't move my legs against the stuff. Uncle Danny's double projected above my head like the broken flagstaff of the lost battalion.

I could see Peggy trotting back toward me, still carrying the skunk. She was downwind, so I didn't have to stop breathing. Maybe thirty yards away, beside a low patch of swamp grass, I saw her halt, crouch, and dive sideways into the reedy tangle. What must have been the earlier rooster clattered up and in my direction. I cocked the double (though I don't remember doing it) and fired both barrels straight up as the bird came perpendicular. He fell like a stone, thirty feet from me on the firm foot of the bluff. Peggy surveyed the situation, dropped the skunk, and ambled around me to the pheasant. Then she lay down, still twenty feet away, and regarded me questioningly.

"Here Peggy, here Peggy girl!" I crooned. I wasn't as concerned to get the pheasant out of her mouth as I was to grab her tail or hind foot to help me get out of the ooze. Peggy didn't move a muscle. Now that she was upwind, her aroma was sort of stifling. She just sat and watched me.

An hour or so of October afternoon passed that way. I began to think about spending the night among the watercress, or at least the time it would take for Jim to look me up. The loose mud was cold. At about 4:30 I heard a feminine "cu-boss, cu-boss" approaching. Mrs. Honeyacre, in the neighboring pasture, was driving in the cows for milking. I gave a couple of loud, embarrassed yells—I was, after all, covered with evidence of my trespassing—and Mrs. Honeyacre duly appeared next to Peggy on the dry foot of the bluff. "Why Dickie Yatzeck, is that you?" She beamed at me, talking and edging toward me on the loose ground, extending the willow branch she used to drive the cows in. She didn't seem bothered by aromatic Peggy. As Mrs. Honeyacre approached, so did Peggy. I was hauled to dry land with the willow branch in my right hand, Peggy's tail in my left, and my uncle's double, running with mud, thrust through my belt.

Peggy backed off a good rod, still clutching the rooster, when I let go of her tail. Mrs. Honeyacre didn't so much as mention trespassing, but suggested a quick wash with the milkhouse hose and a cup of hot coffee.

At the Honeyacres' place Ray was doing the milking so Mrs. Honeyacre bustled about for a mug of coffee and a big piece of hot apple pie. I consumed these, dripping, and quite happy, on the back steps. She mentioned in passing that Ray had always worried about a hunter getting stuck in those spring holes, but she was mostly interested in the news from the city and about relatives. I felt the specter of Honeyacre terror drift away on the October breeze.

After the coffee and concern I walked to my VW, coaxed Peggy into the back seat with a big ham bone—also supplied by Mrs. Honeyacre—and drove to the vet's with the windows all the way down. When told of the situation, the vet was happy to give a curbside rabies shot. I took this occasion to blow in Peggy's ear (while holding my nose) but she didn't move a fang from the rooster.

We got back to Jim's after dark. I didn't say much as he blew in her ear and collected the pheasant. Then he said, "Thank you." I realized that he was talking to me when he added, "This way, you won't have to clean it yourself." I nodded. Fair is fair.

Thinking of Mrs. Barr and the cottontail, Jim's first squirrels, the ancient fear of the Honeyacres and the real Honeyacres, missed shots and the one pheasant, I felt, suddenly, better than I had in months.

September 1985

This clumsy hunt marks that epoch of guilt and rage called divorce. I am old enough to remember when the word was whispered, and then only after the kids had been put to bed. When I divorced, my life seemed put on hold for a couple of years. Peggy and the skunk were like iron nails driven into an old apple tree. I was restored and renewed.

Manning the Hawk

From that time—early in the thirteenth century—for more than four hundred years falconry flourished in Europe. . . . As in the case of hunting and fishing, its attractions as a sport were supplemented by the very material merits it possessed as a means of procuring food. While the prince and the baron valued their falcon-gentle for its high pitch and lordly stoop, the yeoman and the burgher set almost equal store on the less aristocratic goshawk and the plebeian sparrow-hawk. . . . Even the serf or villein was not forgotten in the field, and was expected, or at least allowed, to train and carry on his fist the humble but well-bred and graceful kestrel.

—E. B. Michell, *The Art and Practice of Hawking,* p. 2

The folding fishing chair says "The Udder Uncola" on the back, so you know what its owner, Willard, does. The two of us were trying to catch walleyed pike between interruptions by the lake sturgeon—"gummint fish"—that tended to carry away our Wolf River rigs, three-inch shiners and all, with the aristocratic indifference that defines ancient nobility. These old kings or, rather, queens of the currents come upriver in May to spawn on Willard's rocks. They make a sound like distant thunder. The swamp maple buds were as red as October. Then a peregrine falcon, a silver-blue bullet, flashed low along our bank. (The DDT ban does seem to have brought them back.) Willard tensed—not many farmers love raptors—but I thought, as the falcon flew, of an old acquaintance, Steve King, and of another raptor, Diana.

Steve was an enthusiast, the same who once had great plans for managing coon, and Diana was a red-tailed hawk. When a nest fell along with the diseased elm that a neighbor had been persuaded to cut down for him, Steve rescued a fledgling—falconers call such a bird an eyas—and decided to try falconry. He was prone to momentary passions. He named the young hawk Diana after the Roman goddess of hunting.

"Impatient fellah, Steve King," said Willard. "Wanted to milk a thousand Holsteins at a time. Wanted me to manage a place for him. Not practical. Too much disease. *Nice* fellah, though, or not?" Willard gave me a crooked grin. Steve *was* a nice fellow. A charmer, really. Smile like dark honey, warm grip, he could have sold air-conditioning in Antarctica or, well, hawking to me. When I came into it, Steve had read Michell's book on falconry, converted a dog leash into a creance to fasten the bird, a rat-trap into a lure to teach stoop and strike, and somewhere rustled up a

57

blacksmith's left gauntlet on which to carry the hawk. (Hawks "gripe.") His pitch began with, "Do you know that in the middle ages, before vile saltpeter, *everyone* hunted with hawks? Even *ladies*?" It wasn't long before he had me.

"Even ladies?" Here Steve knew, in spades, what he was talking about. Making his own welcome everywhere, as a good realtor must, Steve had met and charmed the main Wisconsin falconer, a lady who flew a golden eagle, some distance west of the Wolf. (Chauvinist that I am, I count all distances from the river.) He had even taken his wife Ellen there on an Easter Sunday, to soak up falconry firsthand. Now it is a characteristic of large raptors to "mute" or "slice" (void excrement) horizontally, powerfully, rather in the manner of Jinx Whittemore's whitewash pump. Ellen's Easter blue caught a direct hit from the eagle, who ruled the parlor. She didn't even curl her tea pinky. Steve, that one time, was really impressed with his wife's savoir faire. Mostly he didn't really *notice*, wrapped as he was, to the eyes, in the moment's enthusiasm.

That enthusiasm blinded me too, to the degree that I soon had in my house, and in my yard—in my *hair*, really—Steve's beagle, Yuck, his old black cat, Hungry, and a kestrel, a sparrow hawk that one of Steve's farm friends had found stunned in his hayloft after a thunderstorm. ("That was me," said Willard, "I woulda wrung the bugger's head off—he was after my squabs—but Steve had asked me to look out a sparrow hawk fer 'im.") The names of this menagerie were *speaking* names, descriptive, and indicated Yuck's habit of losing his lunch under a hot radiator during thunder and lightning and Hungry's ability, at eighteen, to chase up and catch squirrels in tall trees. The sparrow hawk remained anonymous. Steve brought me all these animals because Ellen had, for once, rebelled. She refused to feed and gentle a redtail, two daughters, *and* all these others. Steve meant me to learn falconry on the sparrow hawk. As I think of it now, his idea was that I would become his austringer, his falconer, and his kennel man to boot. I thought of myself, if I *thought* at all, as a "friend in need." ("Oh, fer a *professor* you're pretty bright," said Willard.)

People may think the "me and Joe" stories that used to be popular in outdoors magazines smell of old long-john democracy. Look at them more closely, and you'll see they're eminently aristocratic, accounts of the relations of masters and serfs right out of the middle ages. "Joe" takes most of the shots. "Me" carries *all* of the game in his jacket, eviscerates it, and delivers the better part of it to the shooter. Baron and serf, really.

Steve, whose last name wasn't King for nothing, did attempt to *man* his hawk. To man a hawk is to "imprint" the bird, as often a duck or a gosling is imprinted to follow the brood hen that hatches it. A well-manned hawk knows, follows, returns to its master. But my "King" had little time to carry the growing Diana on his fist in the manner of medieval falconers. Turberville, a Renaissance expert, described the process of manning, in 1575, as follows:

> Take her on your fist, and hollde her so all night untill day appeare again . . . above all things you must watch her on the fist so many nights together without setting her downe on any perch, that shee may be wearie and suffer you . . . to . . . handle her gently . . . untill shee have altogether . . . forgotten her striking and byting your hand; . . . [sometimes] three, foure, or five dayes.

Steve was not exactly unhurried in his enthusiasms. He lived mainly in a late model Thunderbird equipped with one of the earliest car phones. He had a realtor's promises to keep all over the state. Fearfully inventive, he developed a new method of manning hawks. He surrounded the "block" in his yard, where the redtail perched and was "weathered" or aired, with the wall of an old wading pool, outgrown by his two daughters. On the inner walls of this tank, facing the hawk, hung all of the photographs Steve had of himself. Ellen brought the hawk her julienned beefsteak, and walked her with the gauntlet on her left fist. The two girls disputed possession of her right hand. The hawk "bated" or flew against her leash, and kept up the screaming, the "gak-gak-GAK" which eyases are prone to, never having been taught by a mother hawk when to shut up. As you see, she was never properly manned.

("But he *was* such a nice fellah," said Willard. "It was hurry that did him.")

On infrequent free Saturdays Steve tried to teach the hawk to take steak from a lure: the rat trap pulled on a string or swung across the grass. He taught her, that is, the principle of stooping and striking quarry. When rabbit season opened, Yuck and I had the job of chasing up and delivering rabbits, cut up, Diana's first taste of real game.

Bronze October, and bird season, finally arrived. As I think I said, it had been Steve's plan for me to learn falconry from the book and the sparrow hawk, drive game for him with Yuck, and watch him fly Diana at driven pheasants and ruffed grouse. We spent every spare moment of that month — a down time in Steve's business — breaking brush on the shores of the Wolf. Yuck and I drove promising cornfields and famous grouse coverts. We saw birds. But the flashy cock pheasants were gone long before the relatively slow-starting redtail could get its wings ("sails" in falconer's jargon) humming. Ruffed grouse depart immeasurably faster than pheasants. We were soon down to rabbits.

("I 'member you fellahs coming out after bunnies. More fun than when the hogs ate my little sister," said Willard. "Well, you know the end, but I'll tell it anyway," I answered. "I've listened more than once to *your* stories." "But them is *good* stories," said Willard. And grinned nicely.)

Willard had complained to Steve about a plethora of rabbits. ("Pretty big words," said Willard.) That year he had a cabbage contract with the sauerkraut factory: "Flanagan's Sauerkraut." Flanagan's? Next to the cabbage acreage was a strip of fallow, brushy land, hard to work because the high-tension electric wires marched through it on their structural steel pylons. The rabbits lived in that brush next to the cabbage. It ought to have been a perfect place to train, to "blood" Diana. But redtails are peculiar creatures, and, as we have seen, neither manned nor blooded easily.

When a red-tailed hawk hunts naturally it soars, hangs on updrafts, or perches in dead trees, and waits for, usually, a *mouse* to betray itself. Its height in the air or cruising speed are crucial to a successful kill. To put the matter otherwise, one might say, as Frank L. Beebe, dean of Canadian falconers, does, that the evolutionary position of red-tailed hawks

> is about midway between a commitment to energy conservation and a more dynamic way of life based on a higher utilization of energy. In the training of any of these raptors, this ambivalence is often their most annoying trait. Usually, these are amongst the easiest birds of prey to train to come to the glove or to the lure, but they are often rather difficult to persuade to exert themselves in the pursuit of game. (*A Falconry Manual*, p. 139)

("She wasn't the quickest hawk I ever saw," said Willard. "He *marred* her, Willard!" I said, a bit too sharply. "You know best," he answered, with the crooked smile again. "I can *call* 'em, but I sure can't *understand* 'em." Willard had often whistled hawks close, in my presence.)

We, Yuck and I, beat that fallow field like a bad mule.

("Beatin' never mended a mule," said Willard, "nor anything else neither. Carrots, carrots is the thing!")

That fallow hunk of canary grass and prickly ash lies there in my memory like the block of words needed to conclude this story. Rough, dark, essentially unfathomable on the inside. Bright and brassy outside. But the beagle Yuck, another bumbling serf, sniffed the fallow's edges and then plunged in, and so will I.

The beagle leaned into the bright, brown grass. The tall seed heads rang together like tiny hawk bells. Then he dove, right through the suddenly bloody prickly ash, at the powder-puff tail. I tried to walk, grope, parallel to the now invisible but excruciatingly audible dog. Steve held Diana on his fist as high as he could. He stood, centered, in the fifty-foot square of lighter brush under the pylon. He meant to loose the hawk when she saw a rabbit and bated. He held her up 'til his arm went numb but the game, perhaps alerted by the redtail's still habitual "gak-gak-GAK," avoided Steve's square.

I tried starting Yuck from one side, into the wind, then circled to plunge the brush from the opposite side. After another half-hour, though the beagle was frantic with fresh scent, Diana and Steve had still to catch a clear view of the quarry. When further efforts did bring a lone, maddened cottontail past Steve, he practically threw the hawk after it. Diana, I think, never saw that bunny. Steve's face became as red as her tail, a dark red, but more mottled. He swore, cuttingly, at his servants.

("Well, said Willard, "sometimes some men do deserve the stick. It doesn't make 'em better, but it makes 'em *ponder.*" Willard likes to throw in the odd large word, too. "What he said, then, to you and the dog and the hawk, just wasn't right. You had a decent mother, and the hawk had lost hers."

"Oh, Willard," I said, distracted, "maybe sticks are all there is."

"Not for you to say," he answered.)

Well, then Steve had me *run* through that brush trying to bark like the beagle. He lifted a loosed Diana above his head so that she, creance swinging, perched on the first crossbeam of the pylon, about ten feet above our heads. Finally, he began to bark and run too. It was at this point that Willard fell, choking with laughter, out of the one tree, a seedling apple, in the fallow piece, Steve put his foot in a woodchuck hole and ran his face through a prickly ash, and Diana didn't "stoop," didn't "swoop," but fell, like a stone, on the one rabbit young and dumb enough to pass beneath her. Even I, the only beater upright, couldn't *witness* her success, that "blooding" which was the point of our exertions. The cutting, unmistakable screech of a hopeless cottontail informed me thoroughly, though. Then the hawk rose out of the tall grass with a brown ball of fur in her grip. Steve whistled and held up a still gauntleted left fist. Diana flew right over the fist to Willard's seedling, settled twenty-five feet above us, and ate that rabbit like buttered sweetcorn. She was blooded, all right, but not for Steve. I would never have claimed to have *owned* her.

("He sure did whistle," said Willard.) He had left the vicinity of the seedling, still whooping with laughter from his first experience of falconry, so that Steve might more easily retrieve his Diana. But the hawk wouldn't come to him, even after the cottontail was consumed. Whistling, strips of steak, swinging the rat-trap lure, offering the gauntlet, even dark, honeyed smiles didn't move her. At eleven, when the moon rose, and the hawk "sliced" digested bunny pretty accurately over Steve, he *did* unbend his pinky to cast off the gauntlet, fling the lure, and abandon the "bitch," along with that enthusiasm. I was alone with a sleeping Yuck under the apple tree.

("I was in bed," said Willard. "It didn't seem so funny any more.")

It really didn't. Somehow made finally aware of my serf's status by Steve's withdrawal, I sat on stupidly under that tree. I think that my theory of hunting — see above — took root at about this time, my view of the "me and Joe" syndrome. And, I guess, I thought about Diana and her like, too. When she *did* drop, straight down — thump — as on the bunny, I was there to catch her before she hit the lure. I cut off her jesses — the foot leathers that held her creance — and cast her high into the rising dawn wind. A well-manned redtail, I've read, won't leave easily. Diana didn't even circle, but soared up and off down west, across the Wolf with the stiff breeze behind her.

("She was lucky," said Willard. "If I'd caught her after my pigeons I'd a sieved that pretty redtail." "If you could've hit her," I said. "Even from the hip," he said.)

This austringer left Steve's service at the same time that Diana went west. I'd had it with warm, dark honey. Ellen, of the blue Easter dress, left two decades later. And yet . . . Steve was, as Willard said, "such a *nice* fellah." But terribly impatient.

We went home, then. As it turns out, old Turberville the falconer wrote us a nice conclusion:

> And here I thinke good to expresse mine opinion, that hee which taketh in hand to be a Falconer, ought first to be very patient and therewithal to take singular delight in a Hawke, so that hee may seeme to be in love (as it were naturally) with his Hawke. For, hee which taketh not that delight, but doth rather exercise it for a pompe and a boast, in mine opinion, shall seldom prove a perfect Falconer, but a mar-hawke, and shall beare the bagge after a right Falconer.

July 1994

Willard, with this piece, became a regular feature of my life. Here in the attic, on a window bench, is a small collection of wooden objects—a carved woodcock of dark cherry wood, a mahogany box with a sliding top, an object of beechwood that looks like a tiny banjo. The latter two items are turkey calls made by that same Willard. What he has mostly given me, though, is his confidence—and many a hearty laugh. Somehow these things go together.

Five-Pound Smallmouth

After a bubbly river bank wedding, Diane and I lived for a while on the Wolf River. We were, finally, together, though uncertain how to proceed. "What now?" What *sort* of happiness was to fill our lives forever? I suggested fishing. I was a pretty young thirty-eight.

Diane was working as a librarian, I was trying to write a book—this one—but we had early mornings and an occasional Sunday to squander. I imagined that an eight-foot johnboat was the best place to squander them. Diane, a new housewife as well as a passionate seamstress, had plenty to do: she was, in particular, learning to cook. (She had grown up sewing but her mother, June, had spared her the kitchen chores.) I, home most days, fixed rabbit, woodcock, grouse, and even venison, but all according to the same recipe, with vermouth. Diane, not too surprisingly, pretty soon got tired of the taste of wormwood. Fried eggs on peanut butter toast, my other accomplishment, just didn't cut it. Not even easy over. I was summarily banished from the kitchen.

My new wife's taste, formed by many Florida summers, ran to seafood. The Wolf passed twenty-five feet from our west windows, below a high riprapped bank. So, at six o'clock one Saturday morning I sat across from a determined young woman in the eight-foot boat. As I weighed, and still, unfortunately, weigh two hundred and twenty pounds, while Diane weighs, will weigh about half of that, she mostly looked over my head from the high end of the boat. She possessed, one might say, a certain superiority, even while rowing. I was casting the banks for walleyed pike.

Tadpollies and River Runts, in the color supposedly favored that year by the fish—deep purple—plopped, slopped, and hung helpless in the shoreline willows, snagged on the many deadfalls that obstructed the river, but came back unencumbered by *Stizostedion vitreum*. I said the name aloud, in church Latin. Diane intimated that she was more interested in dinner than in classical learning. "Supper," I muttered to myself.

Every time that we were forced to row—*she* was forced to row—against the current, to recover a badly cast plug, I tried to interest her in the bottle gentians growing beneath the retentive willows. Swatting at swarms of black fall mosquitoes, she soon lost her usually avid interest in flora. She had remained pretty cheery from six until eight, but an awkward lurch—mine—that quarter-filled the johnboat and shoes—hers—with chilly Wolf, led her to a rather grim assessment of my outdoor skills. I bailed, and verbally admired the "Who-cooks-for-you-a!" call of a belated barred owl. "Not me, if you can't do a tad better," was her curt response. I felt, well, less than adequate.

The Wolf, in that stretch north of Shiocton, meanders nicely. It takes eighteen miles of twisting current to parallel the eight road miles to town. The aforementioned snags and blowdowns slow the stream and discourage the seventy-five-horsepower torpedo boats that bedevil the river's lower reaches. Our house, perched on the east bank, was then the only manmade structure visible for miles either way, with the exception of our neighbor Leroy's weathered-to-camouflage A-frame half a river mile north. Blue herons, bitterns, wildfowl of all varieties, and even, once, a flight of American egrets, made, still make that bend comparable to any Everglades. Still, Diane had fished Tampa Bay with her grandfather, watched brown pelicans, brought home sea trout and red snapper. No Isaac Walton, she nevertheless thought that an angler ought to catch a fish occasionally. And the evening meal, which she persisted in calling "dinner," was planned around seafood. At nine o'clock she asked to take a turn with the casting rod.

The time, a while ago, was the end of my bait-casting era. I hadn't yet accepted spinning and thought it dainty and sissified. (I am, you might say, an old shellback.) I said, "I'll be glad to teach you, but it takes a lot of backyard practice. You can't just pick up a Pflueger Supreme and *fling*."

"I've been watching," said the pretty redhead. "I watched my G-Dad too, lots. He didn't seem to have to pick out snarls so often."

"Backlashes," I croaked, swallowing shame.

"Let me try," she said.

I didn't willingly pass her the rod, or do that careful, crouching dance-past to the oars-person's seat. "Let her really screw up, then," I thought. I was not the white knight *I* thought she had married. My first wife had left all feats of woodcraft exclusively to me. For a professor, though Willard has disagreed, I wasn't overly bright.

We finally got ourselves arranged without shipping more than a little Wolf water. As I'd been casting the banks north of the cottage, Diane asked whether it might not be worthwhile to drift south a bit.

"It's all open shoreline," I snarled. "No willows, no cover, no feed—no fish."

"I'd like to try that little pocket on our side of the river. Just down from the house, where the cows come," she said, tentatively.

"Red clay cutbank. Not a bush, not a tree. No decent fish'd hang out there." I ignored the softness in her request, her attempt to make peace. Wrenching the johnboat around with one oar, I splashed grumpily toward Diane's "little pocket." A sewer, after all those cows. No self-respecting sucker would feed there.

"Shouldn't we approach more quietly?" And she smiled nicely. "Won't splashing scare the fish?" It would, if there could have been any fish. I did slow, though, just holding the oarblades still in the current as we drifted even with the little pocket. A small breeze seemed to cast a ripple across the cut in the bank.

"Thank you, love," she said. And dropped the purple Tadpolly right in front of that ripple in the center of the pocket.

"Whump!" And Diane struck back, her hand braking the Pflueger's double crank. The tip of the rod bent right down to the water.

"Snake northern," I crowed—when a broad, greeny-bronze form left the river on my side of the boat, somersaulted until the line hummed against the aluminum bottom and filled my eyes with splash. "Black-bass," the locals call them. I had by now recognized a very decent smallmouth.

The next five minutes were *busy*. At the place where the bass struck, the Wolf is fifty yards across. A hasty smallmouth can cross it as fast as you can turn your head. Diane gave up line, then quickly recaptured slack, as her fish careened. I did my best to keep boat, oars, and head out of the way. I readied the net and had the even greater sense to keep my mouth shut. I found that, questions of love aside, I actually *liked* her, wanted her to have that fish.

A good quarter-mile downstream, in a wider, shallower run, Diane worked the sharp-ribbed shiny dorsal toward the gunwale where I'd low-ered the net. I unshipped the oar, swung the net once, and the small-mouth was between us on the flat bottom of the boat, bronze against rubbed silver. The red eye glowed like a laser. Diane pressed a foot behind the gills and I worked the Tadpolly loose through the meshes of the net with a needle-nosed pliers.

"That didn't seem too hard," she said.

"I'll string him for you," I wheezed.

"Good, thank you, but how about stowing him under my seat? I don't much trust that rusty stringer." Whatever she'd said about the catch seeming not too hard, she was not taking the matter lightly. She knew, a little, what she had done, what we'd done.

That evening, over *dinner*, when the smallmouth, stuffed with onion, spinach, breadcrumb, egg, and thyme, dominated the small kitchen table, she did allow herself a broad smile.

"How's my cooking?"

I couldn't, just then, find words.

April 1996

Since then, after a short stretch in the city (see "The No. 8 Hook!"), we found a white clapboard farmhouse of our own. Diane hasn't fished with me much, lately. She does love to sew while I'm gone fishing, when she's free. However, our offspring David and Sarah simply devour time. When the river god is kind, my catch is often admired. David said, just a while ago, as I flaunted a three-pound walleye, "You're my hero, Dad," then added, "just how long's it been?" Diane asked, "Was it very hard to catch?" And grinned.

The No. 8 Hook!

It was my father's settled conviction that men are reasonable and orderly, while women, though adorable, are fey and feckless. This, plus the iron rule that no. 8 hooks are alone useful and proper for walleye fishing, was my inheritance — along with a set of redwood tip-ups. Their red felt flags were rather motheaten, but they gave good service. I tried to preserve, and even increase this gift of wisdom and wherewithal. I failed. It was Lake Winnebago that destroyed my father's bequest — Lake Winnebago and my wife Diane.

A reasonable man knows that sonar and structure are the keys to successful ice fishing. Reading the reefs leads to fish on the ice. Three of us, new to the big lake, pored over lake maps, studied depths and temperatures, hesitated longer over two-inch shiners than we had before matrimony, and returned regularly, skunked, from the most curvaceous and captivating structures the big lake possesses. Science failed us. Our wives ignored our chilblains. Gradually, shamefacedly, we turned to magic.

We stopped changing our socks. After an initial slug, we left the vodka bottle corked until we had a fish on the ice. When, twice in a row, we filled up on sauger after being stopped by a freight train on our way to the lake, we began to wait for, almost to pray for, freight trains. We were fairly innocent savages. We were all teachers.

One morning, in late March and near breakup, I tiptoed in stocking feet into the pitch-dark of the kitchen to ready the coffee for the "morning run." The kitchen was pitch-dark because Diane and I had a two-room apartment before we moved to Bear Creek, and she was asleep on the sleeper sofa in the living room. The sauger tended to bite at dawn and dark, Pete and Mike were to pick me up at 6 a.m., and we would be stopped by the 6:10 freight before the dash to the hot spot.

I had re-rigged the tip-ups the previous evening, laid out woolies, extra socks, and snowmobile suit, and the coffee was to perk as I dressed. Fifteen minutes before train time the darned stuff finally perked. I stamped over to pour it and came down in the dark on one of Diane's

68

dress pins. She sews a lot — maybe because I fish. "Darn it all, Diane," I whispered in anguish, "can't you ever be tidy?" The loom of Pete's station wagon outside hurried my blind search for the offending pin, and I lost track of it in the sock, in the dark. I left the coffee, pulled on the Sorels, and fuming all the while, dragged my tackle out the door.

My pin hunt had delayed us. Only the distant red taillight of the freight — going west — greeted us at the crossing. Two accusing silences thickened the atmosphere of the station wagon. Darn Diane's pins!

Fog slowed us, but was dispersed by a rising wind at Pane's Point. The road across the lake, still marked by Christmas trees, was lumpy with old, refrozen ice, but we made it to the spot — triangulated by two big box elders and a summer cottage — before dawn. The old hot spot was just beyond a spring break line in the ice, the wind was offshore, but the footing seemed firm enough. Mike and Pete set up tip-ups inside the line. I placed Dad's relics farther out — in the same holes, in fact, where we had caught sauger the week before.

Tip-ups set, we took our ritual slug of Tvarski vodka — it had a bouquet rather like kerosene — and set the bottle in the center of the spread of tip-ups. After this good beginning, according to our theories, only a fish on the ice would pry the bottle open again — and then only for the successful fisherman.

The sun rose. The wind picked up. A very thirsty hour passed, thirsty and cold. With a surprisingly loud "crack," one of Dad's motheaten flags popped up, and I raced, shortly and heavily, for the tip-up. "Shortly" because "heavily." I had come down on the darned dress pin in a new spot. This time, solidly. I sat carefully on the ice, facing the tip-up fifty yards away. I zipped back one leg of the snowmobile suit. My partners' suggestion that I let them ice the fish was rudely rejected. *I* wanted the vodka! I scrambled at the double-knotted Sorel with icy fingers, then cut the knot, eased off the boot, then two socks. The tip-up seemed to be getting smaller, dimmer. The inner sock was pinned firmly to my big toe. I sliced the sock, too. The rising wind now iced both toes and fingers. Planted in the middle of the toe was a no. 8 hook.

I looked despairingly toward my tip-ups. They *had* gotten smaller. The spring crack had become a gulf. The wind, while icing me, had carried off what remained of my inheritance: two lovely, old, redwood tip-ups — one sprung — two newly attached no. 8 hooks, and a possible walleye. It may have been a lawyer — that snaky, eel-like fish — but I doubt it.

A doctor removed the hook before two grinning fishing buddies. I got new tip-ups for my birthday. But my inheritance, and my rationality, had been swallowed by Lake Winnebago. Diane, mailing the doctor his check, dissolved any remaining traces of male superiority with absolutely hypocritical sympathy.

October 1988

This is a testimony to the settled convictions and voodoo rites of those who try to bring home the bacon naturally. It describes more or less accurately their discomfiture and downfall. There is here, of course, no least suggestion that learning took place. I still wait for trains, though they have become few and far between.

Hunting with the Farmer

"My Dad cut this corner post in twenty-three, when we came up from Blue Island," said the farmer. "Rush," said the springer; "whoosh," said the partridge; and I said, "Blam!" And "Blam!" again. Willard is the farmer, that springer's name was Smokey, the ruffed grouse was a red variant, and I missed it twice. That's the down side of hunting with the farmer.

I hunt with time stolen from teaching and family, drive an old car too fast to reachable cover, race the dog to the wood's edge all for a quick fix of mastery, of triumph: the occasional dead bird. Willard farms . . . well, Willard farms to live and lives to farm. His oak and cedar fence posts, his gray geese and guineas, the woods he cuts his heat from and the Charolais cattle that fatten on grass and pay the mortgage: All of these are job *and* joy, means *and* ends. Willard doesn't seem to need my particular kind of "mastery" and looks quite happy with his kind of survival. I'm not Willard, but I am learning. That's the up side.

Willard and Smokey and I are on the edge of a slough, a former channel of the Wolf River. This slough cuts southwest to northeast across the eighty acres of the home place, the first Winterfeldt farm. Willard, as I said already, is the farmer, that is, the person responsible for the cows, young stock, tractors, machinery, buildings, fences, fields, woods, and the mortgage that weighs all. At 2 a.m. he delivers calves, not always helped by the vet. He kills or cures Holsteins with garget or chickens with the pip. He's on the tractor plowing November nights if the ground isn't frozen. He's heard of forty-hour weeks but never worked one. And though he loves his wife, and his kids have turned out "decent," the farm, every rod of it, is his mistress. I want him to trust her to me so I can hunt. He's got his doubts, but has taken a couple of hours to show me this little eighty, this now neglected piece of the larger farm, this land where he grew up.

"My Dad set this cedar post, like I said. (You could let 'em get out a little farther.)" I eject the empties, and something moves me to pick them off the ground and put them in my pocket. I stroke the disconsolate Smokey. Willard tells of the farm, this now tiny bit of land (from the point of view of agrobusiness) which was bought under snow and turned out, when spring came, to be cutover, solid, closely set white pine stumpage. Dad had to rent another place to farm. He'd arrived on the train from Illi-

71

nois with the family and all his possessions. There was no returning. The Winterfeldt family had paid rent, worked the rented farm, and pulled the stumps one by one with mules and tackle. Then built a barn and house, and after three years, began planting this eighty. Dad was killed helping to build a neighbor's barn. Willard raised turkeys and hunters shot some. The house burned and they built another. (When there's a fire, the cutting tools lose their handles — which are replaceable — and their temper, which isn't.) The Winterfeldts bought new saws and axes and knives, as shelter, fuel, and food depended upon such things. Only seventy years ago.

While Willard talked we walked northeast along the south end of the slough, just then full of rushes and cattails and edged by low willow and tag alder. It was a still, chilly, late October day, so still that it seemed a sharp noise would drop the gray–green leaves from the willows. But a square little doe with two shadowy fawns bounced out of them and across the slough without causing an arboreal avalanche and Willard grinned, "Government beef, pretty, too. I wish all *my* stock had twins." I reflected that when I hunt, I just want to shoot a grouse, a rabbit. Then I go home. But these animals and Willard share a home, this farm, and though Willard eats some of them, he feeds them too; they aren't strangers, they're in this together.

We walk on into a stand of poplars, their flat, round leaves yellow as gold pieces, and Willard lets it drop that woodcock, what he sometimes calls "shitepokes," often linger here in fall. Sure enough, the dark marsh soil is stippled with whitewash, Smokey's stub-tail begins to buzz, I look to Willard this time, he nods, and then . . . well, one woodcock for two shots isn't *that* bad. We admire the bright beige beast, the somehow Martian eyes. "Good," says Willard, "do you want to see my woodlot?"

I do, and by now, not just for squirrels. What's wood to Willard? (To me, the hunter, it's cover.) On the north side of the slough now, having crossed the marsh by means of a homemade corduroy path of branches and small logs, we walk a ridge with bigger trees. Ash for axe handles, the kind shaped like a deer's leg, wild cherry for spinning wheels Willard has turned for each daughter, butternut for gun stocks, different oaks for beams and fuel, poplar for the eight-foot bolts the paper mills buy. But it's Willard's cathedral, too. It's quiet, and Willard's voice is soft as he recounts the growth of these trees, for in his seventy-five years they've grown with him, he knows many of them. When his whistle, of which he *is* inordinately proud, halts a squirrel for the shotgun, I don't shoot. This is, it seems to me, the farmer's temple. We walk on.

Into cutover, prickly ash, chokecherry, and a vista of ruins: two wineglass elms fallen crossways, victims of the Dutch elm disease, grown over now with wild cucumber. "Now that blowdown," says Willard, "has held partridge at times." And, as among the young poplars, Smokey swerves toward the moribund giants. "Thrum, hum, Crack! Bang!" and a red bird is kerflop down while a gray variant hums, sputs off in the direction of our corner cedar post. "You made him hunch up," says Willard. "I bet we find him by the bee tree, that broken beech."

Not right away, though. Smokey does start digging into the fallen crown of the broken beech, now a collection of leaves and smaller branches. Willard pulls away boughs to give him a hand, for wounded grouse will burrow into brush piles, even go to ground in rabbit holes. I stand by like a mousetrap, shotgun poised for another flush if we didn't wing him.

Then, and not softly, "BEES!" yelps Willard. "I'm allergic! Back off quick!" He starts, backs, drops bib overalls to sweep out the yellowjackets under his shirt. I see the whiteness of a farmer's back, the rising red of goosepimples on this brisk day, the contrast with the deep mahogany folds of Willard's neck. Miraculously, he gets rid of the bees without a sting. Snorting and shivering he dresses again and, to lighten the mood, I kid him about his "farmer's tan." "Why not, I'm a farmer," he replies. And drops on a stump to take a breather. In a while Smokey strolls up with a gray grouse dug from under the beech. After a long moment to look at the iridescent black ruff, the fanned gray and white tail feathers, we cross back to the cedar post, to the road and the car. "Willard, can I . . . can we go hunting again?" I ask, surprising myself a little. "Just let me know," says a still somewhat shaken Willard.

Evening now, on the back porch of my place, while little Sarah chatters like a red squirrel and the spaniel yawns foppishly. I pick the birds: gray, auburn, beige feathers drift down the evening breeze, a whitey-red skin with goosepimples, feather pores on the grouse's side. Willard! How many seasons left to hunt with the farmer? A good few, I hope.

October 1993

My very first hunting story, rewritten in 1994, this piece attempts to place husbandry and a husbandman in the hunting landscape. Friend Jim is certainly right to assert that Willard strives for mastery too. But Willard's mastery looks like joy, mine like grim competition. I have been known to drag my bloody spoils—when there are any—right through a rival's occupied lecture hall. Mostly, only Willard knows about Willard's triumphs (though he does talk some).

The Rough Local Society

March and April, for hunting types, are given over to watching TV and attending movies about Alaskan brown bears and Zambian cockatoo drives. Evening activities include the banquets and beer bashes of Ducks Up the Kazoo and the Ruffed Grouse Gang. This relatively quiet time has inspired me to establish an organization for the preservation of another endangered species: the Rough Local. The gradual disappearance of this game bird threatens to eradicate all hunting except that of belly-button lint, so I am proposing the foundation of Rough Local lodges throughout the land.

I take this duty upon myself because my buddies always send me into the covert, or lair, to call the Rough Local before the hunt can begin. I am volunteered for this job because I was stolen from my cradle by Rough Locals at the age of five and raised in their warrens. Experience of the growl and lunge of cornered Locals ignorantly approached has made me no worse an expert on such matters than the next man.

First—habitat. Department of Natural Resources (DNR) maps indicate that the range of the Rough Local roughly coincides with the map of the USA (and of other countries, if there are any) except for the pitifully tiny enclaves of cities and public hunting grounds. A territorial creature, the Rough Local chooses, inhabits, and jealously guards a hundred and sixty, three hundred and twenty, or even seven hundred acres of woodlot, marsh, and arable land as a lair site. Like the wild bee, he nourishes himself and his brood on this territory. If his mate is precious to him, his territory is equally so. One violates it at some risk. Most hunting land in our country is within the limits of the Local's territory.

The natural enemies of the Rough Local are many, even legion. Top predators are bankers, the Production Credit Association (PCA), and lawyers. Parasites include city relatives and, most annoying, Urban Slickers. These last are particularly bothersome from late September until January, a period that happens to coincide with the various hunting seasons. Infestations of Urban Slickers, of the Blaze Orange variety, occur most viciously during Thanksgiving week. No one knows why. Both predators and parasites are reducing the population of Rough Locals considerably.

What I want to propose is a feeding and habitat improvement program to restore this greatest of American game species. But in order to approach that goal, one must first learn to approach the Rough Local.

Spring—right now—is prime Rough Local season. He and his brood are caring for black-and-white bovines, much as ants care for aphids, but the Local is not yet immersed in the summer gathering period. The rocks which obstruct his feeding areas need picking. The barbed wire from which he cunningly fashions boundaries needs stretching. His brood is invariably too small to fully accomplish such instinctual activities. Now is the time for the Urban Slicker to approach, call, and offer Saturday assistance. The usual human methods of introduction work with Rough Locals too: a knock (at the *back* lair entrance), a removal of one's head plumage, the announcement of one's name and purposes. Some authorities even suppose that the fodder of Urban Slickers is still provided by Rough Locals.

Once the sniffing ritual is over—and this ritual must be repeated *each time* one approaches the Local's territory—it is a good idea to learn the various calls of the Rough Local. One does this by *listening*. Rough Locals, unlike Urban Slickers, communicate often by what is *not* said. If, for instance, the Urban Slicker should give a throaty call indicating that he'd like to bring his buddies hunting, and the Local does not reply, that means "NO!" The silent "No," along with the shrug, are the first calls that must be learned by the novice Rough Local caller.

My program for feeding and habitat improvement is based upon the preposterous modern view that both Urban Slickers and Rough Locals belong to the same ecosystem and are, or could be, useful to each other. The Slicker who spends five hundred dollars for a shotgun and drives a four-wheel-drive is stupid if he cannot imagine a Friday fish fry for the Local and his mate, a quart of Old Stumpblower if the Local is so inclined, a suggestion that the Local might like to hunt too, and a brace of (drawn) partridges delivered at the rear lair door. Occasional, say yearly, Saturday rock-picking or bale-throwing wouldn't come amiss, either. Such activities preserve the species and improve habitat as well.

Finally, the Rough Local, like his brother the partridge, is interested in survival. He works on the Urban Slicker's hoped-for playground. The Local needs help as much as the fringed bandicoot. As in still hunting, don't hurry the Local, or yourself. If there's wood to pile, or loose calves to herd back to their hutches, leave your gun in its case until you've helped a little. Mainly, approach *this* species of game out of season, not November 17.

Contributions to the Rough Local Society should be funneled directly to your local Local.

October 1988

Coming as I did for many years from town, aiming for a quick hunt, I could remember the (suspended) feelings of my Genesee models for their seasonal city friends. This attempt to explain the attitude of farmers toward "sports" is dippy but not far off target. The following piece introduces Willard to lyric poetry, or vice-versa.

Hunting with a Poet

Poetry is a natural science, except that
It's more comprehensive than any natural
Science . . . I got
The soil the spider forages that
The partridge berry broomed from
That the ruffed grouse ate, gloried in
Till the weasel caught him napping—
The weasel the horned owl whomped in the snow
That became the water the earth needs,
That the partridge berry is fighting for . . .
                    —Jerald Bullis, "Field and Stream"

Jerry wrote that. He was raised in the Ozarks. His childhood trauma was the bite of a copperhead. His youthful joy was the balance of two cased .22's riding behind his father on a trail bike to the nearest good squirrel woods. Our small college rented him for a while as Poet in Residence. Then we—the college hunting and chowder society—introduced him to the shotgun when woodcock season came round. He needed to be reined in some.

His squirrel-hunter's eye allowed him to center on the day's first woodie at fifteen feet: then there were just the two scooped wings on the forest floor and the smoking twenty-gauge hull at the toe of his boot. We thought that a modicum of patience, at least out to twenty-five yards, might lead more effectively to dinner. "I s'pose," said the poet, and then did much better. Still, we had the feeling that we'd "caught a Tartar" as they used to say in Genesee, my only home village.

Jerry's relatively short ignition time told in other academic areas as well. The president's cocktail party for new faculty was much enlivened when this same bard, spurning the red punch, hunted up the host where he'd taken cover in his study and pressed him somewhat curtly for bourbon. Cranberry juice and fizzy doesn't cut the mustard as "cocktails," not even in the relaxed Ozarks. The bourbon duly appeared. At this same party an unusually wordy historian fell unwontedly silent when icy-eyed Jerry, having maybe more than sampled the bourbon, departed abruptly, saying—somewhat purposefully—"That fellah needs shootin'." The history department was pervaded by a contemplative, even brooding silence for the next few weeks.

The second fall I knew him, I took Jerry to Willard's grouse hunting, maybe because his quick shooting was akin to my lack of depth perception. But we had, I hope, more than our lacks in common. As you must know, a grouse gunner doesn't offer his favorite covert to just anyone. But this Ozark poet, this Jerry, so matched Willard Winterfeldt's cross-grained Wisconsin lumber that I didn't feel there was any choice. Willard, wild with overstatement (for our subculture, anyway), went so far as to find Jerry "decent." No small word, here. After a cross between a coffee klatsch and background check in Winterfeldts' kitchen we were blessed off in the direction of Willard's brushy east forty. The poet got a glowing half-grin from the farmer. I was told that I was "allus welcome" because I never did the partridge any harm at all. This, like most truth, was painful. Jerry was nice enough not to pick up on it.

The tag alder piece, made barely huntable by the rambling trails of Winterfeldts' Charolais beef cattle, was nevertheless a pretty fair jungle, even in December. A part-open hard maple ridge, once a sugar bush, formed the south boundary. Here edge blackberries held birds earlier in the season. An east fence overgrown with wild cucumber and a wilderness of windfall elm carcasses separated Willard's land from the public hunting ground. The year before, this cover had produced a lot of wild shots, even a couple of birds slow enough for me. A combined drained slough and rampant prickly ash rise on the north side had harbored flight woodcock and several canny pheasants as late as mid-October. This year, in December, these thorny cupboards were bare.

We tiptoed and stopped, slunk and stilled — in hopes of getting on grouse nerves — through all of these three sides of Winterfeldts' forty, three-quarters of a mile. Only one easy evasion, out of a lone tamarack, rewarded our efforts. That bird, sloping down and east across the public land, seemed to be well on its way to a New York weekend. But in this same time — for hunting dogless can have its pleasures — we'd caught the russet, white-tipped flash of what we were groundlessly sure — because we liked the phrase — was "a big dog fox." We'd been eyed by three pretty does in a gray winter furs, too, and withheld shots at five feckless cottontails. If we were our own bird dogs, we would at least be "straight," though we both loved rabbit pie with mushrooms. "No sense messin' up the woods," as the poet said. We were here for birds. And for the inch of new snow, the silent clarity of paper birches, the bright keening of a red-tailed hawk. Our hunting coats were empty but something else in us was satisfied. It was good to hunt with Jerry, who also sought something beyond dead birds.

The last, west side of Willard Winterfeldt's forty was nearest the house, in sight of the silo with the checkered top, but even more of a

maze than the rest, for it was usually too mucky for the Charolais — now
warmly yarded for the winter. This final edge was a slightly sloping basin
of red willow, tall canary grass, tag alder fastnesses, and small, roundish
openings with bogs and wild cranberry, low and furze-like. We thought —
yes we did — that the Winterfeldt grouse just might have gathered among
those willows, grouped as ruffed grouse will in early winter when feed is
not to be found everywhere. Maybe it was partridge cranberry time. My
point is, we entered that tall red willow patch aware, awake, even a tad too
impatient to void at least the open-choke barrels of our doubles. Our impatience was suitably rewarded.

The first bird flew as Jerry entered the willow copse, straight up, a
ninety-degree turn just a hair above the branch tops, then flat out east,
toward the cucumber-fenced public land. Jerry missed him with the
aforementioned open barrel. Following the flight of that first bird, "trying to get a line on 'im," I was slow to center on a pair of grouse — they
were flying too fast to color code — when they exited *my* willow patch in
tandem. "Bu-blam!" — from the hip — shortened a swatch of twelve-foot
red willow by half, but absolutely no feather fell. "Three birds!" crowed a
pleased Jerry. "The line on your two . . . " but we had, unwittingly or
even witlessly, set off a true ruffed grouse chain reaction. Fumbling in
our neat Bean's coats, dropping yellow light loads in snow just deep
enough to hide them, awkwardly astride red willow tangles, we collected,
for twenty-three shots: (1) eighteen agreed ruffed grouse sightings, (2)
one bloody nose (put the damned gun to your shoulder, goofus!), (3) a
lovely after-battle powder reek, and (4) a set of grouse "lines" which
boxed the compass. We had, clearly, come upon the main herd. ("Pod," a
more acceptable term, just won't do.) Eleven minutes by the poet's heir-
loom railroad watch had sufficed to disperse the throng throughout,
and beyond, the forty. The thunderous silence that followed was not exactly a relief. It was closer to a particularly painful embarrassment. Jerry
said, after a while, "I'd most likely have missed that noisy historian if
he'd jumped with 'em." Between us we'd seen and left practically un-
touched what amounts to a month's ruffed grouse, as grouse go in an
average year. This was, even for me, unusual.

We stood then, in full sun on fresh snow, surrounded by a heap of
twenty-gauge hulls reminiscent of, say, Custer's Last Stand. When my
hearing began to return, partly, the bard with me was chanting:

And once, stepping out of the ravelment of timber into a glade,
With a rivulet sprinkling over a cliff to the hollow beneath,
Turkeys burst up all around me, wingwallops like shotgun blasts,
Iridescence of wingback and neck tingling with sunlight,

And one great tom—an easy thirty-pound gobbler—
His double-beard swung black in the air like a scalplock,
Fell away from the flock in a long, slow drift to the valley
Of woods below me, merging at last with shadow a mile
Away. . . .

I liked that. Still do.

As you may have noticed, I said we left that herd "practically" un-touched. Jerry thought that his last bird might have hunched up under the shot, the usual sign of a nonmortal hit. That grouse's line was, of course, clearest because most recent in his mind. Otherwise we might have gone equally sensibly in any direction. Anyway, the poet set out for that north line of slough grass and prickly ash. Following Jerry I came, after him, into a fifty-foot clearing, kind of circular, dotted with clumps of brown foxtail on bogs with open, snowy dips between. In about ten min-utes Jerry found tracks, sharp and fresh, leading to a pile of old elm branches left here when the dead elm was logged for fuel. I kicked the end of the pile when Jerry seemed ready, then shot when he said, "Take 'im!" to me, or to the red bird that had whooshed out the other end, sort of like a bottle rocket. "So-whump!" the little clearing echoed and I saw, unbeliev-ing, this bird falter and drop over the horizon of surrounding prickly ash. "I've got a line! Why didn'tja shoot?"

"Cause mine was GRAY!" the poet chanted, and "Hold that line!" Swiftly deconstructing the brush pile he found, under the bottommost limb, the freshly dead gray bird. Grouse use cover, dead or alive.

Ignoring, for a good moment, my red prey, we admired the lustrous blue-black ruff on Jerry's bird. Just looked. Didn't talk. "A quiet angel flew by," say the Russians. It was—always is—that sort of a moment. With the right buddy. Then we went after "mine." (Has anyone ever owned a ruffed grouse? Eaten—certainly. Owned—never.)

In due course we came on a second set of fresh tracks—four steps—in a second opening in the prickly ash. These four sharp small prints led right into a rabbit burrow in a low, snowy bank. I lay down, reached in—to the shoulder—and got tailfeathers, tail, a wing, a head, and like a vet birthing a calf, I pulled the red bird out head first. "Don't just roll over, do they!" said Jerry, looking down at the flapping half-angel I'd made in the snow. "What about the Ourada now?" Two grouse was, this day, just right.

The Ourada was a corner bar a quarter-mile south of Winterfeldt's. But, again, before we left, we admired this dark-red phase ruffed grouse, so rusty that even the ruff glowed coppery. As it happened, both Jerry and I were redhead fanciers. "Hope some of that mess we left for seed are sib-lings of this beauty," he said. "More'n likely."

In the fullness of time — we had lingered cleaning the grouse for our host Willard, who admitted utter surprise; would be, he said, "flummoxed!" — we reached Club Ourada. They sold beer, there might have been brandy, there certainly was music: Kenny Rogers. We had followed "The Gambler's" first three rules. When, after maybe three boilermakers, though it had seemed to get dark fast, Jim Ourada called over toward our pool game: "Partridge hunters to the phone!" we followed Kenny Rogers's last injunction. Saying only, "They just left!" in unison, we trotted out the door. That was, plainly, a redhead on the phone.

August 1995

Let the deer swim in the mist of the dawnbroken wood,
Let the partridge bulk alertly, craning its neck from the tamarack, ready
   for blustering escape at any second;
For I'm pleased with the partridge, the acrobat of the poplars,
The one who keeps a tree between himself and danger,
For his sophistries of exit dispense lessons unbeknownst to him,
And I sign my presence by his booming out of the pines . . .
               Jerald Bullis, *Adorning the Buckhorn Helmet*

Leroy

I didn't hunt or fish with Leroy, ever. As a young man he had shot a running rabbit with a .44–40. The rabbit cried out, as rabbits in despair will. Leroy never hunted again, though all his seven woodsman brothers did. When I knew him, he kept the fire going in a riverside A-frame, fileted fish on my infrequent lucky days, and made popcorn or fried sidepork on the others. He was, then, grown up enough to be beyond the boyhood diseases of fishing and hunting. Still, he promoted blood sports by welcoming killers into his cabin on the Wolf River and allowing that atmosphere of wet boots and old long johns that leads to hunter's talk, which Faulkner considered the best talk of all. Maybe it is their baseless belief in freedom that makes the talk of woodsmen good.

Leroy's A-frame talk often turned on the Trilateral Commission: the Rockefellers were using it to take over the country. They would rule from an island free of nuclear contamination in the South Atlantic, free of contamination because the South Atlantic winds blow counterclockwise. Or, sometimes, OSHA was the enemy, particularly pole-axed for a brochure sent to (and, of course, paid for by) all farmers, which explained the dangers of falling into a manure pit. Leroy had me do a dramatic reading of that one. He taped it, and played it to the cows as he milked. But these mild paranoias always seemed as much an attempt to hunt out and flush my own bigoted liberalism as real statements of fear and loathing. Leroy, the scholar, had a healthy suspicion of mere scholarship, its rites and beliefs. He no longer hunted game, but he still hunted.

"When you lose your self-sufficiency, you lose your freedom." I first heard this at the Club Ourada, nursing a beer and a grudge against my wife and watching Leroy—whom I didn't yet know—beat Lee Nelson at pool. He was talking about the expense of raising your own field corn. "It's cheaper to buy it nineteen years out of twenty." He lit a Camel. This was twenty years ago.

Somehow, the next day, we were in his woods, close to the river, cutting down a dead "swamp maple." When the big tree fell he brushed off the stump. Then he began to speculate about what had been going on when that tree was a sapling, a hundred and twenty or so rings back. "I don't know," I said, "but Aldo Leopold might." "Oh," Leroy muttered, as near crestfallen as I ever saw him, "you read the book too?" "Yah," I blew it off, "but not often enough." I wanted to blunt my discovery of Leroy's sources. But he went on. "Since you know books, could you find me a copy of Berry's *Farming: A Hand Book*?" Leroy liked to set other people's beagles on his rabbit tracks. "Sure." I'd, then, never heard of Wendell Berry. I got him the book. Ten years later, in an apparent reference to a niece's wedding which he did not attend (Leroy seldom referred to the subject of his interest directly), he quoted Berry's "Mad Farmer" line: "at weddings I have gritted and gnashed my teeth . . . ."

Leroy was a bachelor. I heard a nephew say at his funeral that there had been a girl once—long before they all became women—but I never heard Leroy refer to her. He did not demean women in the A-frame conversations as men alone sometimes do—a fishing cabin needn't be a locker room after all—and he was generally "courtly" with them, though that might seem an odd word to use for a man who lived, died, and was buried in a checkered shirt and "stagged" woodsman's pants. I remember the grace with which he told my wife—yes, that same wife, I haven't made *that* big a collection—that she had taught him the use of pumpkins by making one into a mousse with the addition of sugar and Jack Daniels. At home—he lived with Willard (the one and only) and sister-in-law Arlene—he exhibited the countryman's usual assumption that housework was women's work. (I am not describing a saint, you know, just a normal good man. As Stanley Crawford asks in *A Garlic Testament,* "Have you actually figured out how to live a clean life in a dirty age?")

Self-sufficiency was, then, a later—maybe *resulting*? —passion. Beef cattle—Charolais—that would fatten on home grass, not boughten grain, young stinging nettle's asparagus taste, dandelion root coffee, or roasted rye, the orchard perhaps most of all, which he sprayed thirteen times each summer from a wagon that looked like an oval wine barrel on wheels. (It had to be soaked, like an old rowboat, if it was to hold spray.) Ultimately Leroy and another brother, Paul, got their own, portable sawmill. Steps to freedom, I guess.

Now I gradually realized that all of these artifacts of self-sufficiency had to be gathered or tended or sharpened by brother Willard and/or his wife Arlene. They only issued from the brain, and books, of Leroy in theoretical form. There *was* some work that he would undertake: the spraying of the orchard, planting apple, pear, black walnut, and white spruce, and, in the fullness of time, making wood. But these were, really, his pleasures. Everyday barn chores and garden work were not. Leroy was a scholar–farmer, and, of course, the neighbors knew it. He was as proud of his two years at River Falls State as if it had been Stanford.

I think that there is a place in the world for Leroy's ways. He did what he loved to do and avoided that aspect of the work ethic which can poison the best labor with righteousness. That first fall that I met him, he sat one tree over, dropping O'Connell ("Canal") Reds into a worn canvas apple picker, and almost chanting, "An apple is a living thing." Meanwhile he demonstrated the little twist and push toward the trunk, along the limb, that stresses the tree least. He would throw me a hacked "Red" from the top of the tree and proved indeed that "the crow-pecked ones are sweetest." He was especially pleased if he could leave a wasp in the cavity for me to find — not in any mean way, just to see if the wind and the sun had put "the professor" to sleep. He kept a couple of old Ribeston Pippin trees alive — with spells, I think, for he drove nails into them — because they were English, exotics, and he had read somewhere that they are often given as gifts in Yorkshire on Whitsunday. Their skins are like leather but their flesh is nutty and sweet. He called them "Ripskins," but he knew them well.

Again, making wood, he sniffed the fresh sawdust like incense, told of lethal swamp maples that would turn like a top — in all the four directions — before lunging to catch the sawyer as they fell. He had, further, as with the "Ripskins," his own version of taxonomy, when he called the Balm of Gilead tree "bum-gilear," the "bum" resounding like a heavy trunk bouncing against resilient ground. Willard and I loaded most of the wood, but enjoyed Leroy's almost musical accompaniment. He hadn't a doubt in the world that when a tree falls in the forest, it makes a "bum" whether we're there or not.

Not being a churchman like the rest of his fellow citizens, Leroy's community activity, when I first knew him, was the spraying of all the apple orchards within his rather long reach, once he had finished his own. Creeping along crooked 187, which parallels a particularly twisty bit of the Wolf, on a Minneapolis Moline tractor kept running with parts cannibalized from twelve others, he was a block and a blight to all impatient drivers; that is, to all drivers. In a rusty pickup, inspecting his township when *not* spraying, he was even more of a beam in every motorist's eye, because he *could* have gone faster. But he would check the straightness of every corn row, consider the provenance of every strange cow. After his funeral I watched a white Lincoln move him, with stately grace, north toward the town cemetery. "Best set of wheels he ever rode on," I said. "Hell," said his friend Beanie, "that's the fastest he ever traveled, too."

Moved, probably, by Socrates' assertion that the alternative to governing is to be ruled by others worse than oneself, Leroy ran for, and won, the town chairmanship. In that role he found road work for indigents and delinquents, oversaw snowplowing, arranged for machinery repair, kept the cemetery records, fought or ignored the demands of central government, and chaired board meetings. His official robe for this new dignity was a gray cardigan that he commissioned and my mother knit. When, after ten years, he was voted out of office, he had kept some of the powers of decision local and left, as his monument, a paid-up new town hall. This is now the site of weddings, reunions, funeral feasts, and sheephead tournaments, a northern equivalent of an Italian piazza. Maybe, like his pickup, he was thought to move too slowly, too conservatively, for what had been farm country and now was largely bedroom real estate. He had, I think, genuinely enjoyed his rule.

During the last five years he spent most days, except in deepest winter, reading in the A-frame, when he was not conducting his leisurely inspections of the now wretchedly governed township. He stoked the pot-bellied stove. He dozed some. When there were boys around, especially when they should have been in school, he tried to teach them how to fish. As I, at some level clearly still a boy, rolled an illegal lake sturgeon back into the river after detaching the hook, he said, maybe reproachfully, maybe reminiscently: "They do taste good, though." He could remember the days when sturgeon sold for fifty cents apiece from a farmer's wagon. Long time ago.

The last day I saw him he had picked a gallon of blackberries behind the barn foundation in the Deer Creek hunting ground, and found there a wild crab apple tree. He told me that it is fruit that would put hair on my son David's chest and tossed me a couple of deep green ones. Thoreau says of these apples:

> The cows continue to browse them . . . for twenty years or more, keeping them down and compelling them to spread, until at last they are so broad that they become their own fence, when some interior shoot, which their foes cannot reach, darts upward with joy; for it has not forgotten its high calling, and bears its own particular fruit in triumph.

When Leroy died, dropped in Willard's living room by a stroke as he was finagling a potato-digger for his nephew Mark, I was nowhere about. But I know the sound he made as he fell. "Bum-gilear!"

July 1994

Willard's younger brother. Mirror image and, of course, reversed. Grim-looking and butter-hearted, he loved boys and apple trees — not always in that order. As the pumpkin incident suggests, Diane and I were still living on the river near Willard and Leroy. A truckload of cordwood, a heaping platter of venison steaks, countless Canal reds were the least of their presents. They welcomed us into their lives. Our kids, too. David is happily convinced that Leroy haunts the A-frame.

Fall Tree

For Leroy Winterfeldt

The standing clamor of the October maple
in windless air is silent as some stone.
Where shall we learn such soundless, smokeless blazing
except just here, chilled, breathless and alone?
I would approach and drink the yellow vibrance
but, not equipped for such a draught, I halt,
amazed, high, stilled by leaf-glow's pungent liquor
and find words too much, not enough, and in default.

November 1993

Diane and I sometimes buy and plant a tree rather than ordering flowers
when a friend dies. So we set an O'Connell Red in Dennis's mother's yard
when Ray, her husband, went; another in the yard of a colleague, Pete,
when his mother passed away. Leroy was *such* a man for trees that I'd like
to plant this maple here for him. He had enough "Canal Reds" of his own.

Manna

Phyllis was shelling peas under the big arch of morning glory that she plants every year for shade, and because it's pretty. She lives in the trailer house next to her son Dennis's place now that Ray's passed away and Dennis is the farmer. "In the field," she said, smiling up when I asked for Dennis. "He's a pretty good worker if he doesn't get dragged off fishin'." She smiled again, though, for she's accepted me as Dennis's buddy and throws a mean trout line herself, being from up North.

"I'll get you a cup of coffee. Dennis should be in shortly," and she rose — for the ten thousandth time? — to pour coffee for a neighbor, carefully setting the pea pan in the shade of the steps, watching herself on the trailer stairs, now that she's seventy. But her cheeks are still like Ribeston Pippins.

We drank the coffee there on the steps, under the nodding morning glories. The deep blue blossoms knitted about the antlers — "deer horns" — trophies of Ray's preternatural hunting skill, nose for game. He'd been the son in his family who brought in meat in the thin years of the thirties in Jump River, the provider, sometimes, of "government beef," as venison somehow was called. I spoke of him, Phyllis's ten-years-dead husband, Dennis's father. Something in my tone, though the words were fond, made her look up from her peas again.

"Ray *was* a hard man when *you* knew him," she said. I sputtered, but she raised a reassuring hand. "You ain't said nuthin' wrong about him, but your thinkin' peeped through. He was hard and his life was hard. And he made my life hard, too, and bitter sometimes. But there was reason in it."

I said that I was sure there was, since denial hadn't shielded my thought. "Let me tell yuh though how we came to marry," Phyllis offered, after a while. She got up first and went into the trailer to fill our cups again. "Ray came from nuthin' and his father, Jake, was a hard man too. From boy up, Ray wanted to farm. His dad was a logger and Ray knew the trade, but he loved cows. Every year in high school — in the thirties — Ray'd buy or beg a heifer calf to raise up. He hoped to get the start of a herd that way. But every year his dad would sell the calf in the fall, for fuel money or maybe for mere meanness, but he *was* always short. How Ray did want a herd, though!

89

"When we were both seventeen we started to keep company, at church socials and such. Our folks didn't hold with dancing. I believe it was the one time in my man's life that he wasn't mostly thinking about a farm. Ray was logging by then, working as a saw sharpener, but the pay wasn't much. My dad, mother bein' long dead, didn't want to lose my hands around the farm, I guess. He *said* that 'til Ray had a farm of his own, we ought to wait. Dad had ten Holsteins and sixty acres, no bad place, then—nothin' now. Ray's folks, dad, mother, and five younger brothers, was against the marriage because they thought me not good enough for Ray, and maybe didn't want to lose their best hunter. Anyway, we run off and got married in Eau Claire, skiied into town on the last of the March snow. We was pretty warm, then.

"Now we needed a place to live and we needed to eat, and Ray's saw sharpening was done for that year when the frost broke up. His dad, or mine, got to the woods boss and Ray wasn't hired on for the spring log drive on the Pine and Chippewa. It looked as though we'd be hard put to make it through the spring. Ray'd likely find field work on a farm in June. I don't rightly know what kind of work *I* expected to find. I'd only ever worked at home, and Ray surely didn't want me workin' in someone else's house. Anyway, we were up against it, or so it seemed.

"As it turned out, Ray had thought ahead for us. As we skiied back from 'Claire, on our wedding day, he told me about a cabin near the logging site that a Chicago man didn't come to any more maybe because of the hard times. There was a wood stove and a hand pump and bunks. Ray'd already hung a deer in the lean-to. We had a home to go to, anyhow. For now.

"Well, 'now' lasted three months. We had venison in March, and bread that my soft-hearted baby sister—she'd married early—tramped over with every week. Three big brown loaves in a towel, and she always left the towel, too. Still, bread and venison did get some dull. But, we were young and independent, and that was worth a lot.

"Now Ray *was* a hard man, later. The fight for a farm made him one. But he was just as young and soft as I was then, though maybe a mite less ignorant. When I was plain scared on our wedding night he just held me, gentled me, let me finally go to sleep. Like I say, he wasn't always as hard as when you knew him. That sense, the knowin' enough to be patient with me, and the stubborn war with our folks, held us together, I guess. Now later his dad gave in some, and my folks did too, when they saw we meant to stick it out together. But right then it was bread and deer meat, and in April fiddle-fern to go with it, and then nettles. Nettles kind of taste like asparagus.

"In May, after two months of this, it began to rain. Great, tearing thunder storms, lightning like nothing I'd ever seen, though Ray said that from what his dad told of the first war, the artillery must have been like that.

Every weekend, it seemed, the sky just opened up and beat on our old cabin, the Chicago man's place. And it leaked. The wet wood didn't want to burn in the wood stove. We were a couple of miserable water rats, I can tell you. And even fresh deer meat — Ray got another buck between storms — didn't seem to help. But then, then — there come a sunny day. We looked out of the cabin door in the early light and the ground seemed white, or off-white at least. Late snow, we thought. You'll never guess what it was."

"Frost? Dew?" I tried.

"No. Morels. Ray said they must be what the Bible meant by 'manna' in the wilderness. With bread and meat, fiddle-heads and morel mushrooms, we just feasted. And the morels kept up all through May. Then, whatever his dad or mine could say, Ray was asked to cruise timber for the next winter's cutting, and my dad said he'd stake us to vegetables and canning supplies if I'd come over times and tend the garden for them. That gave us a good toe-hold, and we've gone from job to job, then farm to farm. Renting, then buying, working in town for cash money sometimes, milking a hundred Holsteins when Ray passed away. He got kind of callused climbing that high ladder. You couldn't often see the young man, the patient boy he was when we married so young. We had our spats, and sometimes we didn't speak. But every April or May, depending on the year, he'd bring in a mess of morels for supper at least once. And we'd smile. We'd always said — between ourselves o' course — that Dennis came of those morels, of that 'manna in the wilderness,' and I believe he did. He's turned out just as foresighted and patient as that same young Ray. Anyhow," and her voice, which had been low and confiding, came brisk and cheerful again, "here he comes traipsin' back from the field, finally. You two go along and fish. We'll have mushrooms, store-bought mushrooms with your trout, if you get any. It's late for morels." And Phyllis winked at me, from under the morning glory arch, as we left. When we got back, with the trout, there was fresh blackberry pie, too.

February 1993

Another "Rough Local" story told by Phyllis, not me, since she experienced it. But she told it with hot coffee on a cool day, garnished it with
wild blackberry pie, and then it became my experience too, a gift from up
North, a story of material survival, subsistence, the primary attraction of
the rural past. I bought my clapboard farmhouse from Ray and Dennis.
"Burn 'er down!" said Ray, when he heard how much insurance we'd been
able to get. Ray was a real subsister.

Thy Neighbor's Pheasant

"Kuck-uck-uck-uck. Blam!" The shot was northwest of me, behind a screen of popple. Near the line fence. Dennis, the farmer, has given me hunting rights here if I'll keep an eye on the fences and the woods. No one but me has a right to hunt here. Smokey, the black-and-white springer, has already headed toward the shot. I follow, righteously indignant.

I need the righteousness. I'm supposed to be fixing birthday dinner for my wife, Diane. She's working days at the cabbage factory, I nights at a bean cannery. We share the chores. We do this to remodel the frame farmhouse we bought here. But the insulators from Norgas have driven me out of the house with the whine of their blowers. I don't intend to go back 'til they leave. After lunch. I'm not really hunting; I just took Smokey and the twenty along "in case." My conscience is relieved by the clear duty to oust a flagrant poacher.

The poacher is, maybe, fourteen. He has an old .410 single. He is hung up on the wire of the line fence as Smokey licks his knee. He didn't see any posting signs, has always hunted this eighty, was looking for a partridge that got up in the middle of the hay stubble and might have come down here. He must have missed it. I let him know that the hunting rights here are mine, that he's no longer welcome, and that partridge neither frequent open hay stubble nor crow.

It's only after he turns away that I remember. I told just such unlikely stories when I was fourteen. My bad conscience about Diane's birthday dinner is not eased by this eviction. Rights. Neighbors. That line is harder to draw than a line fence.

The kid is out of sight when Smokey gets hot at the east end of the popple screen. We both chase south, he dives into a patch of red willow, and I arrive in time to rescue him from a crippled, angry cock pheasant. The boy *did* hit the bird. As I wring its neck, I'm of two minds. Fall plowing and fence clearing have made pheasants rare in our neck of the woods. It's not really my bird. But the boy *was* poaching. And the bird would have gone to the fox if Smokey hadn't found it. It would make one hell of a birthday dinner. I take the bird.

By the time we get back to the house the insulators have picked up

93

and gone. It's 2:30 and Diane will be home at 5. I clean the bird and hunt up a recipe, not without qualms of guilt. The bird belongs to the boy with the .410. We need sherry, whipping cream, and asparagus, if possible. Smokey and I get in the rattle-trap pickup and head for town.

Returning with the sherry, whipping cream, asparagus, and a bottle of André's best champagne, we run into our first retribution. A cabbage truck passes me going uphill, a late wasp stings me on the left hand and I hit the brakes, sharply, for both reasons. My curse is punctuated by a heavy "thunk" under the hood. A cloud of white vapor frosts the windshield and the engine temperature takes a sudden jump. We torkel to a stop on the hilltop. My battery, not properly secured in the cradle, has flopped forward and broken a radiator hose. The antifreeze is all over the hot motor. My left hand is welling to cantaloupe size. Smokey is nursing a bruised nose.

There is a farm on the hilltop neighborly enough to lend me a pail of water. More neighborly than I seem to be. I can shorten the hose and re-clamp it. I can drive with one hand. But there's not much time left to cook the pheasant.

Back in the kitchen, I set out the bird—nicely singed—a cup of whipping cream, half a cup of sherry, and the rinsed asparagus. Then I open the top cupboard to reach the small pressure cooker. Retribution again, in the form of a pound or two of new insulation which has filled the cupboard through cracks in the plaster. Increasing my velocity I find the vacuum cleaner. The howl of the vacuum is accompanied by more verbal exercise as I clean Smokey, myself, the bird, the cooker, the asparagus, and, with some difficulty, skim the cream and sieve the sherry. Into the cooker and onto the stove. Basta!

Diane, as it happens, gets off work half an hour early, but my "hunting" story amuses her until the champagne is cool and the pheasant and asparagus done. We eat the stolen bird—quite well cooked—drink the champagne, and, feeling pretty jolly, decide to turn in early. We even scamper up to the bedroom.

Now Diane has a favorite white chenille bedspread. From better times. It gleams in the middle of the unremodeled, not to say "shabby" bedroom. But not this evening.

There is a good inch of gray insulation on the bedspread, the floor, the bureau, the clothing in the open closet and even in the lined-up shoes. A small hole in the plaster on the south wall has somehow admitted what looks like a full bag of the stuff. "I'll call the kid and hunt until we find *two* pheasants for him," I think.

Now we are tired and somewhat under the influence of the champagne. We shuffle through the gray stuff, fling back the cherished chenille, and roll in anyhow. I nudge Diane. She says, "Kuck-uck-uck-uck. Blam!"

January 1984

The first story I ever sold, this one incorporates whatever approach I could muster. Everything except the boy-poacher happened on the one day. Together, the experiences make one large pratfall, illustrate the mixture of doing and dumb suffering that country life meant as Diane and I settled into our "five acres and independence." The short hunt, a there-and-back-again rhythm, wood's edge to clapboard, and the tension of nest-building and hunting inclinations, as well as the problem of rural neighboring, will appear again.

The Pipes, the Pipes Are Calling

I spent Thanksgiving Day in the septic tank. In Wisconsin, Thanksgiving always falls in the middle of the nine-day deer season. Since I am one of the 650,000 who buy deer tags here I should have been, had planned to be, in my tree stand Thanksgiving morning. But I wasn't.

Opening weekend it rained. I watched a doe slip sinuously by twenty feet away and eighteen inches off the ground half an hour after the 6:30 fusillade. No doe tag. I had managed to miss the deadline for filing. At my age—fifty—she was no great temptation. A wet grouse the size of a six-week pullet grumped and shivered under my stand, too. I started smoking pretty early. No bucks. The grouse and I sat in that rain for two days, on and off, and neither of us made any thundering noises. So the next day off, Thanksgiving, with new snow on the ground, was full of hopes.

Thanksgiving eve the septic backed up into the basement and nothing would drain or flush. My wife, Diane, inured to the seasonal fever, said I should go ahead and hunt. She and the kids could do without plumbing for the day. A last scrap of decency made me change out of hunting gear in the morning and trade the shotgun for a shovel.

First find the tank. It's somewhere on the east side of the house. South and west of our place the first shots were resounding as I made another exchange—shovel for pick. The ground was frozen. I had hoped to be hunting by noon.

Cloudy but bright. The pick didn't contact cement for two hours. Since Thursday is late in the season, the first drives were beginning by 9:30. I broke frozen clods, then shoveled down to cement by 10. The growls, yodels, hoots, and screeches that my neighbors make driving the edge of the Lebanon swamp south of me are sort of irritating. I miss my own attempts to sound like a hunting horn. Where the Hell is the trap to the septic?

It's a large tank, I discover. Circular, eight feet across, and the trap is *not* in the center. By noon I find it, though. Blaze orange figures dot all the horizons of this flat country. I am sure, given the volume of the barrage, that one of them must have shot the six-pointer, a fat devil, too, that spent the fall bedded in my east field. Damn it to Hell. The trap's stuck.

Pick and shovel are traded for an arrangement of two car jacks and a steel fence post. After several ringing collapses, this rig does pry up the trap door, a hundred-pound cement block. The septic is full. The pump truck operator is sure to be hunting today.

My submersible pump, which sees lots of service in the porous basement, takes a couple of hours to lower the liquid under the blanket of septic debris. The Murphys across the field are dragging a suspiciously fat-looking deer north out of the swamp. I doubt if I'll make it to my stand for the last hour of hunting.

O.K. The tank admits six feet of my painting ladder now, and I climb down in hip boots. Six inches of cement should at least keep the slugs out. The eight-inch pipe to the basement seems to be plugged. I need a long stick. With an awkwardly long piece of hardwood trim, relic of an abortive remodeling effort, I ram at some unseen stoppage. Kind of hopelessly. Bill Murphy rattles up the drive in his pickup to borrow a block and tackle—they want to hang up a big six-pointer. I fetch the gear nastily, then hammer some more at the plugged pipe while he tells me how he done it, in technicolor. I don't refuse a Stroh's from his truck.

He dances off—a successful deer hunter can even dance in a ten-year-old pickup. I hammer some more, than feel the plugged pipe release. When I'm too slow to get out of the way, the spray hits me four inches above my hippers. Dripping with my very own slime, I stand in the yard and watch Bill and two sons raise the buck. Their box elder is a quarter-mile west, but it seems like it's right under my nose.

Diane signals through the kitchen window that the sink's draining. Victory, I guess. And then. And then, riding a sharp west wind, sixty whistling swans cannon over the house a hundred feet up. Bugles! Brass! Beauty! I will never move back to town, ever.

Bill brought me a yard of sausage when he returned the block and tackle.

July 1984

The all too gradual learning of maintenance skills, the temptation to cut and run, shotgun in hand, is at the center here, too. Yet I can remember a certain proud warmth when the cement port of the septic tank finally lurched loose, again when the pipes began to flow. The *doing* is what counts. (Or is it the bugles of the whistling swans?)

Dave's Buck

I didn't get along with my brother-in-law. I voted for Mondale, he voted for Reagan. I taught, he moved from factory to retail business. I—I thought— barely made ends meet. He bought new cars and took his family on trips. Maybe the worst of it was that my mother doted on Dave's success and generosity but called my second wife by my ex-wife's name. There was, as they say, "bad blood" between us. His, or mine. But here he comes in a hunting story, big as life, as much to my surprise as it would have been to his.

The implicit rivalry generally kept us apart, but one fall, near Thanksgiving, my sister Sue called to ask if Dave might hunt deer with our party. His brothers, all hunters, made fun of him some for never having shot a buck. Could he come and try his luck with us? I couldn't politely say "no," was tempted to say it anyway, chickened out. He could come, I said, shortly.

Dave showed up the evening before Saturday opening, in a new Buick. (I was driving a VW bug without running boards. They had rusted off.) He came without a gun, in an orange team jacket and tennies, wearing a red baseball cap. The weather *was* warm, but it kind of shook me when he said he meant to *hunt* like that. Could he borrow a gun?

The guys in our bunch, an odd mixture of professors and farmers, wear hunter orange outfits, Sorel boots, and spend weeks—and dollars— practice-shooting, oiling gear, getting ready. Here Dave would take any old gun, wear any old outfit. He made our seriousness look silly. His casual attitude graveled me—as if I'd been friendly to start with.

I have an old Ithaca pump, open bore, bead front sight. Damned if I'd lend him my deer gun. Dave agreed, grudgingly I thought, to try out the Ithaca. Offhand, at the regulation fifty yards, he managed to put a hole in my old burning barrel, near the bung, and said that that would be fine. I was too grumpy to press him to shoot at least one group. We went in for a brotherly beer and then, since wake-up was at 5, to bed. I didn't sleep well, tossed, muttered, 'til Diane told me to roll over and shut up.

Opening morning the whole party was ready to take up hunting stands an hour and a half before sunrise. We'd walked the farm the weekend before, chosen our posting spots, kind of danced the pre-hunt dance of memories and lies. Dave, of course, knew nothing about this, didn't

99

even inquire much. Pete, colleague and hunting buddy, explained that in party shooting, if you got a chance at more than one deer you should take it—though no one expected Dave to down even a doe fawn. We would all be within shouting distance of each other, we wanted the tags filled, no one was too choosy how. Most likely he wouldn't be able to pull the trigger even once. The guys were savvy enough not to remark on his tennies and team jacket, though someone, seeing his hat, did ask what base he played. "Shortstop and general clean-up batter," he said, kind of cockily, I thought.

Where should he hunt? Every good spot was covered, acquired by years of custom; people traditionally hunted the same spots. The farm lies just east of a big blueberry marsh, now overgrown, and rises about twenty feet higher than that swamp. The neighbors drive the swamp, the deer come east after a couple of hours of playing tag in the brush. We hunt a fence line, a couple of small sloughs, a stand of pines that the deer pass when they leave the marsh. Our spots lie pretty much in a north–south line to intercept them. Way over on the east edge of the farm, two forties—half a mile—away from the swamp, is a small wood, a field grown up in red willow, the refuge the deer head for. I posted Dave in front of that, on a pretty open fence line. Told him, as "clean-up man," to shoot whatever we missed. Didn't expect to hear from him at all that day. Forgot him, in fact.

Well, we occupied our usual spots. We heard the usual spatter of "booms" in the dark, then the thicker downpour when opening time finally came. But no shots from the blueberry marsh to the west and, after three hours of sitting, no sightings of even small deer. We got together for hot coffee at the house about eleven—I'd forgotten to invite Dave—and bitched. The Wisconsin DNR couldn't manage a herd of goats. The blasted bow hunters had killed all the bucks in the early season. The deer were bedded down in the still unharvested corn. Last year's hard winter had starved most of them. No one felt—and on the first day, too—much like driving our few patches of wood and brush. If the swamp didn't produce, why should our scanty woods? We were a sulky bunch but did, of course, after enough coffee and lies, get ready to drive a couple of likely spots. We piled out of the kitchen, decided who'd drive the small woods, who's stand to intercept the deer, where. Then, a single "bang!" East. Dave's direction. Reminded us that "the baseball player," as he'd already been nicknamed, was still there. He *was* my brother-in-law. No one said anything worse. One "bang!"

Though it's twenty feet higher than the marsh, the farm is pretty flat. From the back of our house you can see Dave's fence line, the woods and brush behind it, even an orange team jacket. With binoculars which, real quick, everyone had to his face, you could see Dave clearly. And, loping right past him, heading south, a big deer with horns like a hat tree. "Shoot, shoot," someone yelled—and then I realized it was me—though, at half a mile, Dave probably didn't find it too urgent. He stood there, even lowered the gun, let that deer right by him without a salute. Then he walked back in the direction that that swamp buck, that frigging *trophy*, had come from. Why? To find its damned *bed* or something? All of us started trotting toward Dave's fence. We had to know what happened.

We found out. In the fifteen minutes it took us to cover that half-mile, Dave had gutted, messily but efficiently enough, a smaller, but very decent, fork-horned buck. The big buck's pilot fish. Dave's slug had taken it just behind the ear, come out the other cheek. It lay seventy-five yards, plenty long shotgun range, from Dave's stand on the fence line. "Is it a keeper?" Dave asked quietly, maybe even sheepishly. "Hell, yes! But how could you let that monster buck lollop right past?" Dave stood up from the gut pile. "Well, I know Pete said to shoot, fill another tag, but it seemed—piggish. One felt like enough, I guess."

Everyone didn't agree, but I saw, gradually, that I'd have to take another look at this brother-in-law. I thought—long and hard—as he told in words, as our Indian predecessors showed in dance, how it had been done. He had stood and stood, got colder and colder, rolled on the frozen grass to warm up. A couple of times even. Slapped his arms as far as he could around that team jacket. Took off the tennies and rubbed cold toes. Stood again. Seen us go to the house but thought he'd better wait, since no one else was covering the last fence line. Clean-up batter. Then he'd heard— behind him—something like a little train whistle. A snort. Turned as slowly as he could. Seen the fork-horn.

"I wanted the skin whole, like yours in the bedroom, for Kelly. My daughter," he explained to the others. "So I aimed for the head. Took a breath, let it half out—just like in the army. I don't remember shooting, the deer just dropped. Before I could move, the big one rose up out of the brush, from behind this one I guess. Looked me over, ran right past me, not all that fast. That's when I thought, and I do hope it's all right, that two would be piggish. Like I said. Hope you're not mad."

We took turns dragging Dave's buck. Cut off his shirttail, Dave's I mean. Clinked beer bottles. He had the hide tanned with the hair on, for a rug for Kelly. Kept the horns on the wall in his store. Never needed—he said—to argue with his brothers any more.

I guess those horns were on the wall when Dave was killed in his store, in Phoenix, this winter. Shot down when he tried to stop a holdup. It probably wasn't very sensible of him. He'd kept a derringer in the store. The holdup man caught both slugs in the breast-bone, but his .44 magnum killed Dave instantly, the police said. Dave never paid much attention to guns, just to straight shooting. And not being "piggish." I wish that my mother had doted on him for the right reasons.

January 1995

In our first years here on Blueberry Road hunting was generally out the back door; Ray and Dennis let me hunt the half-section — 360 acres — that they farmed or left in woods here. There was lots of edge. The deer hunting crew, mixed locals and professors, tended, as in Dave's story, to spend a great deal of time drinking coffee and discussing the approach to hunting. Ray, impatient with this, once left the group, took a seat on a stump near the woods edge, shot a deer, gutted it, and dragged it out before the rest of the group had decided how to apportion itself for the hunt. Anyway, we hunted right here; I can see where Dave dropped his first buck if I look out my skylight. Dave, of course, I can no longer see, at all, except as suspended in memory. A good man whom I came to appreciate pretty late.

Two Hunters and a Fool

Hawk-shadow silences the red-wings in the
slough. They don't shut up for me.

The sun is an egg easy-over in the west. The little flight of mallards is a good sixty yards over me. But the old, worn-shiny L. C. Smith has thirty-inch barrels. I shoot. That is sky-busting.

I'm on a fence line woven with wild grape halfway up a hill. The slough is at my feet to the south. Pyos, the young springer, rolls down to intercept as one of the mallards—hen or drake, *I* couldn't tell which—begins a long, slow half-spiral into that slough. The duck disappears where tag alder and cattails meet on the west side as I pound down after the dog and circle to the point of impact, as best I can. The mallard's not there.

Pyos chases out into the standing corn before I get to where the dead duck should be. I call the blasted rabbit-running cur back to the alder–cattails edge, where the water starts. There's an east wind and he should scent the damned duck. But it's November, last day of season, and there's floating slush in the frigid water. I pitch Pyos in. He swims and hunts.

He paddles, snorts, and sniffs, but his heart's not in it. He checks out the small slough for maybe fifteen minutes, circling back toward me questioningly but making another tour through the cattails when I yell. No duck.

I do have the sense to towel him off with my hunting coat. He shakes himself again, takes his earlier track into the cornfield after the rabbit—and a big greenhead bursts into wobbly flight from a puddle in the corn, heading toward the south fence line and our house. I am not ready—the sun's been down half an hour anyway. I've already wasted one bird by sky-busting, and now the season's closed. I trudge after Pyos.

He runs ahead south, down the cornrow, and comes out five minutes ahead of me on the stone-piled fence. Heads west, toward the house, tail a blur and nose down. Rabbits again, or maybe he smells supper, even against the wind.

And then he stops, lunges behind a piece of Waupaca County granite, and brings up a flopping drake mallard shot, it turns out, once through the chest. A tough bird.

Now it is time, as we walk home, to think about what sort of a fool

I've been. What sort of a fool haven't I been? I sky-busted a mallard at sunset, took Pyos off of the duck's track to make him swim in the freezing slough for twenty minutes, misread the drake's clumsy jump from the puddle as that of another duck, and cussed the dog out twice for rabbit hunting when he picked up the trail again. The greenhead was a tough and wily adversary. The only reason he's in my game jacket now is that Pyos is a better hunter than I am. Hell, I'm no hunter at all!

I am not always so thoughtful, but I woke early the next morning still bothered by my shot and its results, bothered about what kind of a hunter I really am. I stood by the stove for a first fix of coffee, just at dawn, and saw new snow out the window. Then I got my lesson again.

A tiny dark-velvet shape ran along my west line, thirty feet from the house. After it came a white swirl in the snow and an inch of black fur brought up the rear. The dark shape disappeared in the swirl. Intrigued, I went out in unlaced boots and long-johns to find a mole track, a weasel track, and three drops of blood in the fresh whiteness. Pyos, and the weasel, are hunters. I am a more or less foolish bystander.

March 1987

Back in Dennis's slough and out the window of the white clapboard I was taught this lesson. We don't "hire" our dogs, they don't "work" for us, at least not in the usual sense. If we're sensible and lucky, they become both companions and perceptors. If we are awake, they teach us. Against all reason, they love us anyway.

The Running of the Deer

Waupaca—A Marquette University psychologist says deer hunting can satisfy a variety of needs. . . . "The simple answer would be that they go deer hunting because they enjoy the experience, but there is a more complex answer," Stephen L. Franzoi said as Wisconsin hunters took to woods and forests for the gun deer-hunting season which opened Saturday. . . . Franzoi said four general areas in which needs are satisfied in deer hunting are achievement, affiliation, aggression and the rite of passage.
                                                —*The Post Crescent,* Appleton, November 18, 1984

I'm a deer hunter as well as a professor. I'd like to translate Dr. Franzoi's "achievement, affiliation, aggression and the rite of passage" into a particular deer season in my home county. First "achievement" and "affiliation."

We hunt a wooded eighty, and another hundred and sixty acres of cornfields and grass-grown ditches. Regularly, making late hay, chopping, then combining corn, we see the heavy-beamed buck we call Hartford. I just drive tractor; Dennis is the farmer and gets to keep the books and deliver calves at 2 a.m. He sights the big buck more often, wants him more than—in place of?—balanced books. Fights down the temptation to "do" him with the .30–06 the week *before* season. And wonders, over coffee and pie at Jansen's, if he wouldn't rather see the buck run "free and clear."

Opening morning Orion's sword belt is as bright as the Big Dipper, it's nippy, and Dennis leads me and John, his cousin, to the wooded west-pointing promontory of the eighty. He settles us in tree stands we repaired two weeks ago. Then he climbs a large box elder in the marshy middle of the point. At 6:30 a gradual trickle, then a cloudburst of shots east of us. Silence at 6:35 and one shot, from Dennis, at 6:40. The wheeze, or snort, of a buck—hit or missed—and the snap of thin ice under hooves. I can see Dennis in his stand and a grayish, elongated form heading southeast toward heavier brush, upwind. Then Dennis climbs down, circles maybe fifty yards east, and a large deer of no clear description catapults, somersaults out of three-foot canary grass. Another shot and "Dick!" "I'm not coming down unless it's him!" I call, knowing how slim the chances are that just Hartford walked under just Dennis's tree ten minutes after opening. "It's him or his brother," says Dennis.

The big buck is, finally, still. Not a two-foot, but a sixteen-inch

spread, knobby, heavy "swamp buck" beams, seven-inch tines and brow
tines, and a perfect, singing eight-point balance. Dennis is quiet now,
watching the buck's hindquarters relax. "I'm not sure I wouldn't rather
see him running free," he says, again. We drink coffee, eat a little choco-
late, and Dennis guts the buck as I head back for my stand. I'm *damned*
glad Hartford didn't come to me first. I'm an "achiever" too, but Dennis's
smile, though troubled by the wish for a dead *and* free-running Hartford,
is wider and more relaxed than I've seen it for five years anyway.

I guess that covers "achievement" and maybe "affiliation": roughly,
being buddies, too. From the positive side at least. Now "aggression." Dennis's and my feelings about shooting Hartford were certainly mixed, but
the unexpected triumph of that early moment in the season surely outweighed our regrets — for then. The downed buck — that we later cut up
into roasts, chops, and sausage meat in Dennis's wife Deb's kitchen —
was a solid, completed act, aggressively completed, and a relief from the
uncertain wars with Mastercard, the weather, and the mortgage. There is
other violence. A week after season, hunting partridge with the springer
Pyos, his circling excitement led me to the spectacle of a buck's testicles
hung in a low prickly ash. That, I think, is another kind of aggression. I
detest it, but feel it occasionally myself. Only not toward deer.

Toward deer hunters, rather — again, that season. The day after
Thanksgiving I had my kids — David, three, and Sarah, five — with me behind the chicken house cutting up old barn beams for fuel. Their mom was
gone to the sales. We were dressed in orange and behind us were three
houses and two barns. Occasional distant shots enlivened the day. I plied
the Swedish saw and the kids played fire-engine on an old thistle-header.
Suddenly — the word is too lumbering for the experience — shouts, shots, a
viperish hissing of slugs through goldenrod, toward us. Hunters in a
slough two hundred and fifty yards away had spooked two does, it was late
season, and they weren't paying attention to their surroundings. I yelled —
Hell, I bellowed — at the kids to "get down," and they looked at me, stupe-
fied. I raved northeast at the hunters. They stopped in their tracks. Their
ancestors, their mothers' honor — all fully amplified — were thoroughly dis-
cussed. The shivering weakness in my gut as I led the kids to the house —
that was a forerunner of "aggression," all right. I thought of those hunters,
and *their* private parts, when I saw the buck's testicles in the prickly ash.

And Professor Franzoi's "rite of passage"? I remember *my* first buck.
I was thirty-six, in the middle of a divorce, smoking a Camel and cold
clear through when he walked by at seventy-five feet and I, almost too
late, raised a redone 7 mm Mauser to take him through the lungs. Twelve
years of deer hunting. Too many skunkings to count. But thirty-six is too

late to "become a man." Maybe I never did. Chris, Dennis's nephew, did though.

The same morning that Dennis shot Hartford, about an hour later, Chris, starting his second season, saw a partridge flush out ahead of a running doe. He had a doe tag, the doe slowed as she came out of the patch of dogwood that had sheltered the partridge. Chris aimed, opened and shut his eyes to clear them, breathed in, forgot to hold it, then shot with the shaking pump. The doe flattened, hopped, bellered. Chris ran up and shot her again, at ten feet, in the neck. Then he sat suddenly in a patch of frozen corn stubble and wept. When Gardener, Dennis's father-in-law, came out of his tree to see what was up, Chris said, softly, "I want my slug back. I want her alive again." I guess that's sort of a "rite of passage."

Dennis's "achievement" in killing Hartford put him back in a world of tangible success, though roughened with regret. I felt "affiliation" when I realized what a relief it was that Dennis and not I had shot Hartford. I saw, then felt, the black reality of "aggression" when I came upon the buck's testicles in the ash tree. Chris grew some — experienced a "rite of passage" — when he realized that the death of the doe was real and irremediable, and that a man might cry over such things. We will all, most likely, hunt again — go from bacon smoke to wind-whipped tree stand, to the moment when you hit, or miss, with closed or open eyes. The best of us will maybe realize that hunting is a mixed pleasure. Like life. And that it teaches us about ourselves and life, too.

I have tried to translate Professor Franzoi's theory into experience. That is, after all, the only thing to do with theory. But I find that two important things have been left out. Stupidity — mine — and death — another's.

My buck, this year, was standing between two seven-foot rows of corn in the middle of a field we were driving. He was facing away from me, into the wind, and I thought at first he was a fawn. Perspective and excitement made me think him thirty yards away. He was farther. I walked toward him and saw the small sickles of a yearling's horns. Then I got scared — of losing him — held the rib of the 20 over/under on the back of his head, jerked instead of squeezing, and shot him through from ham to shoulder, at sixty yards. He thrashed away, out of sight, and though we — mainly Dennis — carefully followed the blood trail, we retrieved "my" buck only because hunters south of us saw him, dropped him, and willingly handed him over when we came out of the corn. I had shot excitedly, stupidly. I am fifty-one years old.

Death, finally. I went shopping the Monday of deer season and felt a stillness in, of all places, the supermarket. I had the kids with me, joked about baby-sitting when I'd rather be hunting, and got a red-rimmed, stony look from Nancy, an old friend at the checkout. Then she said, "We lost Bob this weekend." Bob Schonwalter, a young father, a factory worker who moonlighted at the store to support a young family, had been killed by a ricochet opening day. I knew him vaguely, slightly — a smiling face, a willing arm to carry the dog food to the car. What good thing can be said about deer hunting to balance Bob's death? To Nancy, to his family. Nothing balances death, not even its inevitability, when the victim is young, healthy, and engaging in an apparently unnecessary sport.

Here I can only speak, like a professor, in theory. For myself, I hope that I will use all the care of which I am capable, quit hunting when my stupidity or inability endangers others, and meet death as resolutely, if not as uncomprehendingly, as the buck does. Whether a responsible member of the human family has a right to this attitude about hunting I'm not sure. I am especially not sure that I can live up to it.

November 1985

The above is an attempt to translate from sociology to hunting talk, theory to practice, human terms to "merely" animal ones. I suppose that the rejection of hunting for enjoyment, insistence upon a "more complex answer," got me going. I become an even more obvious bigot whenever the suggestion of arcane knowledge spawns a spanking new vocabulary.

Pyos

His paw prints must be, under this new April snow, still everywhere along the edges. When he died in the zero weather of January I felt a sudden numbness, short-windedness as after a forward fall over a branch, concealed by that same new snow. Now memories, and thoughts sprung from those memories, outline first the exact shape of loss: the shape of a blunt-nosed liver-and-white springer. He didn't die like a dog in a ditch, but at work on my thought-blunted instincts. Of course he never considered this. His teaching, like much good teaching, was by unconscious example.

Twelve years ago I returned from a camping trip in eastern Europe to find that my springer Gus—a real charger of a pup—had died of an infected abscess diagnosed too late. I went, then, to share my grief with Dennis the dairy farmer. (You've met him on his "eighty.") North of Dennis's barn, in one of his new calf pens, was a springer pup. "Whose pup is that?" I asked distractedly. Phyllis, Dennis's mother—who told "Manna"—often gets stuck with the calf care. She looked at me with friendly annoyance. "What do you *mean*, whose pup?" It dawned on me that Gus had been replaced.

I named him Pyos Denisovich—Russian for "Dennis's Hound"— though he was not, strictly speaking, a hound, yet. It is his paw prints that now, under the new snow, thread the little woods, marshes, and sloughs for three miles round about my house. It is his silent teaching that I find, now, readied me for his death.

I am no trainer, though I am sometimes a teacher. Ignorantly I taught Pyos, during his first October, to retrieve newly harvested cob corn. He developed a hard mouth from the delight he took in chewing the corn off of those ears. No amount of scolding, or beating, could break him of biting wounded, active partridges, though he would bring a downed bird to Dennis unscathed. I always had to race him to the landing site of a winged bird. He had no other faults at all. And *this* fault, even, taught me over the years of won and lost footraces to beating wings the reality, the finality, of cause and effect.

Once, on a bird hunt in public lands that were formerly muck farms, farms drained by deep, wide ditches, I beat him with a red-willow switch for crushing a young grouse. Shortly thereafter he swam a six-foot ditch to retrieve a stone-dead woodcock and—although he shared the bird dog's frequent disdain for woodies—he eyed me calmly and ate it right up, as I raged on the other side of the very deep and muddy ditch. I never beat him again, and he never ate another bird, but I had learned that I had to live with the hard mouth that I had caused.

A real sportsman, a gentleman bird hunter, might have replaced Pyos at that point, and trained his next dog better. Perhaps with grouse wings attached to a length of two-by-four with nails in it. But I had hopelessly fallen for Pyos by that time and I'm not a gentleman hunter anyway. I learned to live with his hard mouth as with my own lack of depth perception: I ran footraces with Pyos as I do better on crossing shots than on straightaways.

Over the ten years of life with Pyos the energy crisis, inflation, and two children all tended to reduce both the range of our hunting and the budget of money and time that could be allotted to it. My adaptations included a closer attention to the wishes and needs of neighboring farmers and a return to hunting out the back door. We seldom drove anywhere to hunt, but increasingly zeroed in on the rabbits and coons that plagued our neighbors' gardens and sweet corn patches. Pyos adapted by becoming a passionate coon hound, though I could never hunt him at night because he didn't learn to bay on the track. Still, the special howl of my otherwise silent partner alerted me to the presence of maybe a dozen coon a year, as did also the coon's usually bad-tempered snarling as I stumbled closer.

I say "bad-tempered" but, after all, I hadn't been awakened in a sunny canary-grass clump by the banshee howl of a springer trying to be a redbone. Anyway, once we took up coon hunting Pyos paid his own way, and my license fees, with coonskins. He crossed some human line unknown to him from hunting pet to working dog. Mainly, though, he was my professor along the edges, and taught me to see, a little, what he was always aware of.

Although we mostly hunted—and missed—ruffed grouse, the presence of which called forth a controlled, fierce electricity in Pyos's movements, I learned gradually to distinguish the kind of scent he was on by his demeanor. Hungarian partridges were signaled by short, high leaps in several directions, pheasant by a pressing, high-nosed sprint along a single line. A low-bellied sneak meant woodcock, while cottontails were the only game he barked at. He told me about a deer by a guilty look over his shoulder and always returned, after his puppy days, to a quiet "No." He was straight, as they say, on deer. His stance gradually taught me what kind of game and, therefore, what kind of a shot could be expected.

Pyos chose the cover, too, though I was five years learning that his nose was better than my educated guesses. He was, after all, born and bred for the job while I had only my overplus of brains to guide me. Approaching red willow, grassy swale, or tag-alder clump, he taught me where I might generally expect to find the game I sought. Of course he always hunted into the wind until now I do too, as naturally and happily as he did, without having to choose to. Whether his particular high-hearted gaiety in the chase goes on in pups he sired, or is maybe just a general springer trait, I hope that some of it rubbed off on me. As Mr. Roberts would say: "Sure it did."

Finally, thinking of those paw prints disappearing with the tattered snow of another spring, invisible on the shaggy April pelt of the hay field behind the granary, I see his brown, warm, but quite objective eyes. Dogs are said to adore, and maybe he did. But what I remember is a patient brown gaze after the third miss and the calming cigarette, or, in passing, as he brought a long coon backtrack past my waiting stump: "O.K. Let's go." "O.K. Pyos. I'm coming."

January 1988

He was the third and last of my English springer spaniels: Smokey, Gus, and Pyos. I have not been able to bring myself to replace him. My hunting friends choose pointing dogs, English setters, or Brittany spaniels, for the advantage of clear warning when a bird is present, and for beauty, too. I shoot just as badly with or without warning, and love the sudden berserker rush of the flushing dog.

Up North

Last summer my city students began to make fun of me for my vague use of the term "up North." What does it mean? How would you find it? Why not say Wausau or Park Falls or Rhinelander or Eagle River? Wouldn't that be the kind of precise language that I am always demanding of them? Yes and no.

"Up North" is not mainly a place, but a condition. One must, indeed, be able to smell pine trees, but *some* kind of conifers grow all over Wisconsin. Woodsmoke helps, especially if it smells like incense because of the lichen on the bark, but the room must be impregnated with it. The knobby feel of the bases of deer horns, the "thrum-whoosh" of a partridge, and, of course, the demented wail of a loon. Gray herring gulls from Superior heralding a Canadian blow. But those are the trimmings of the Christmas tree, the gift that "up North" means.

It means, then, a mood and an atmosphere, not a place. Because its location varies: Shawano was "up North" 'til I moved near there, then Park Falls took Shawano's place. It means a dream, now more and more lost, along with the ozone. Gordon MacQuarrie, in a Wisconsin-famous story where he cried, "Just look at this country," doesn't just mean "look" but also "remember," "feel," "live" this country. Oh, cripes, how to explain "up North?" I'll try, here and now.

The best of my growing up — as you've heard before — was on a sixty-three-acre, thirteen-Guernsey farm in Genesee village. The farmer, Art Bloom, had been a saw sharpener in the pineries around Ladysmith. From his stories, punctuated by the slap, then softened "plush" of milk in the bucket as he milked Polly, "up North" meant the grainy silver edge of a newly sharpened crosscut, the spurt of red sawdust from cedar, dirty socks, and "Daylight in the swamp!" I sure wanted to get there, for the feeling of male competence in his voice, for the unspoken love of that particular earth. "Up North" was the Promised Land.

Just last fall I got up North again. I went by car and Greyhound and van. To Stevens Point, to Wausau and Rhinelander and Minocqua and Park Falls and Glidden, to Spillerberg Lake and Torrey Lake and Chequamegon Bay. And then home again to Bear Creek, like a bear to its scratchy den under a blowdown, inside Wisconsin. I thought I'd died and gone to heaven. Or, as Mary Lynn Whittemore said when she first rode the gas-lighted, wood-stoved old Genesee train to Waukesha: "God, ain't it beautiful?"

Right now I hear a February wind. The piled-up Canadian cold has broken loose, shattering our week of thirty-degree weather. The whistle of this wind on the naked maples brings my last up North pilgrimage sharply in focus. By contrast, the ride up was archetypal October, crisp and mild and cobalt blue with the lower rim, the world, a leafage of ocher and crimson and chrome yellow. Wausau was a rumply patchwork quilt of hardwood hills under a blue bowl. In the bus, since I wasn't driving, I was looking, and the gradual increase of conifers, the flattening of the hills, the greater frequency of little roadside estuaries between lakes—where one expects, toward evening, to spot a reeking moose (or even a woolly rhinoceros)—gave edge to the feeling of North. A fifteen-minute rest and snack stop, maybe in Rhinelander, included a quick bowl of chili. Up North chili always seems to have noodles in it. It was good, anyway. As we kept on, the swooping, gliding flight of moustached ravens replaced the flapping of crows. Granite boulders substituted for limestone outcrops. Things, natural things, are different, other, up North. Hairier. More lichened. Older. Harder.

But I try to be a hunter sometimes, and sometimes a fisherman. Up North is the place where such doubtful habits can be most fittingly— most secretly—indulged. That's how it feels anyway. Concrete bucks and papier-mâché muskies have increased up there, but in some ways it's easier to understand advertising in the north. Most of the year it's harder to live there. Most of the year it's winter.

Fishing. Yes. I was invited up North to fish with one of the oldest and best of buddies and his budding sons. Certainly a lot of the charm of the place, an acute delight of being there, is the pretense that I'm a real fisherman, an outdoorsman, with the single goal of catching a humongous muskie or a great hook-jawed chinook. When I go to work I teach—what? Life?—and the unseen money dissipates into an inchoate fog of bills. But up North I have a black graphite rod, a "five of diamonds" spoon, and, maybe, a steelhead, to *eat!* No more, but no less. I have a very definite aim, and since this goal is attained, or not, by physical activity, by throwing the spoon out with the wind say twenty-five times an hour for six hours, I haven't much time for lolly-gagging, thinking of other possible goals. This is a relief, a great part of the pleasure. I don't want every possible sort of joy, just a fish. And then, maybe, another.

Walt met me in Glidden, near the biggest Wisconsin black bear, stuffed, and we went to the lodge on Torrey Lake. His sons—my God! old enough to fish muskie—had hot chicken soup ready and went to bed as we sat down after dinner to pluck a wild turkey. Talk. Lies. Memories of a sixties' grouse hunt in a Model A Ford. An argument about whether the painting over the stone fireplace was of a dog or a weasel. (One of the boys got up from bed to take down the painting and settle the argument so that he could get some sleep.) We, chastened maybe a little, went to bed then too. But the feeling of *two whole days* of northern fishing ahead, an endless time—that went like a bear through buckwheat—was headier than any bourbon. The lakes, the bay, were *here*, right here before us, as we hit the bunks that first night. Thoreau wrote of the wood thrush: "Whenever a man hears it he is young." The smell of woodsmoke, the play of shadows at the back of the fireplace, will do it too.

The first glorious day didn't start so well. We had drunk Wild Turkey bourbon the night before, and now Walt was fixed to the bed by the famished turkey *buzzard* (101 proof) which had roosted on the bridge of his nose and was pecking at his eyes; he dared not move, could not see. Blind, he gave me directions to Spillerberg Lake. The muskie suckers had mostly escaped, but there were two left. Walt's directions, or *my* buzzard, led me and the boys on a long, rough, stumpy, and ultimately mistaken detour down a logging road that dead-ended when the van perched on a sharp granite outcrop over a profound looking swamp. We backed up and backed out and did ultimately find the lake by taking *the next* left turn. At noon then we were wind-trolling the north and south sides of the lake alternately, walking the suckers over reefs and through pickerel weeds. I dredged with a Suick. The boys, having realized that I was no gentleman before whom they needed to pretend to be nice, were having a knock-down drag-out fight over whose turn it was to row. Just then one of the sucker bobbers submerged. Too quick a retrieve brought us a well-lacerated sucker, but no muskie. Then we began to *fish*. With adrenalin running like a brakeless gravel truck we worked that angle of the lake again. And again. No response. Blown.

When we finally looked up from our labors, one of the boys spotted a bum beckoning from the landing. Matt said, "At home in Sioux Falls, that would be a child molester." Ignoring these suspicions we left our sucker-drowning and picked up Matt's father anyway. In the next two hours we had three hits on suckers, but half-hour waits didn't get any hooks into any muskies. We reeled up one line, we saw the fish—a keeper—holding the bait as a black lab holds a folded Sunday paper. But just *holding* it. Not munching. The helplessness in the boat, the absence of fishing wisdom in the two "adult" men, and the fine, sonorous zeal of Matt and Mark, made the air electric. But the muskies would not be turned on. We saw fish. We had fish on. We got skunked.

Back at the cabin, van unloaded and steaks sizzling, we decided that it was too warm for muskies to really hit. That might have been the reason. And then again, the acute angle formed that night by Mars, Venus, and the moon could equally have been our problem. But the steak was good, the bed just right, and at midnight Canada sent us a north wind and good handful of cold rain. Dawn gave us a pristine, shiny new day.

Hans, who runs the resort, had agreed to take us up to the big lake — Superior — to Chequamegon Bay, to try for chinook and steelhead. The season on lake trout had closed the day before except, as Hans said, for the Indians. Now Hans *lives* "up North." And he *lives* the motto of that other guru of mine, Leroy Winterfeldt: "When you lose your self-sufficiency you lose your freedom." Hans hosts, guides, logs, taps sugar maples, carpenters, plumbs, filets fish — oh, everything that can be done he does rather than buys. He can tell the pines and the oaks and the lichens apart and he knows that the Canadians use house cats to bait their fisher traps, and he's a damned good shot. Hans is what I've secretly, secretly wanted to be — along with every other Wisconsin male I've ever known. Why does he resent the Indians' special seasons, spearing rights, life *outside* the white man's law? Canting liberal that I am, I don't think *racism* is any kind of an answer at all. What is?

Hans wants one law for everyone, if there must be a law at all. I feel that he would like, as I would like, the utterly self-dependent life, the money- and plastic-free life that the Indians once had. He maybe envies the Indians their extra helping of self-sufficiency that the old treaties granted them. But I don't really know. I only feel, intuit, that part of this "up North" business is the desire to slough that modern life which is so far removed from pine-needle duff and eagles and to become, or at least to pretend for a while to become, what the Indians used to be or, maybe, never were: real children of the real earth.

Anyway, Hans took us to the bay. He offered — quietly — to motor troll, but smiled when we all preferred to run up North against that Canada breeze and float back past the Sioux and Onion river mouths, casting blue-and-silver Daredevils and little Cleos and red-and-yellow jacks of diamonds for browns and steelheads and chinook. These fish spawn upriver in October. I asked how long it takes the eggs to hatch, what chance the fry have for survival in winter Superior. Hans said, "They're tough. Some make it." And he knew what he was talking about.

I caught my chinook early — although not in the first line of this piece, in the way that you are used to. The fish sets the hook here, not the fisherman. If you are too snappy, you lose him. A light thunk, a slightly steeper bend to the graphite, and if you keep the line taut and the rod up Hans will net you one. The salmon was small, three pounds maybe, but the hook of the jaw, the silver, arrowy shape declared him a cousin of the more famous Scottish and Norwegian fish. My first, and the little fish easily outweighed a couple of February depressions. If I knew how *that* works this would be a better piece. A big enough fish, then.

We cast all day, twenty-five times an hour, not counting a noon beach break for good bread and ham, Walt's favorite sardines and pickles, coffee and cookies, a beer and maybe a joke. Bluebills were already working the water in decent flocks and we'd seen eagles. Another boat passed with a carved wooden cormorant on the high prow, a curly red-haired dog, and a white-blond fisherman. The whole rig smacked of Vikings and primitivity. Wilderness, wilderness.

Now Hans is a professional. His jokes, his "talking it up," his prophecy of a "feeding frenzy" due right now, make you see killer whales in the middle of the continent. Because he is an expert his reputation is always on the line. He's supposed to do what only God, Manitou, or the barometer can do: provide fish. Toward dark, as the eagles became less frequent and we had, still, my one lousy salmon for five rods, he must have felt discouraged, though his voice never gave him away. But then, just like John Wayne to the rescue, fish backs like horses' manes curvetted under that clean sky, through those steel waves. The boys picked up two chinook bigger than mine, and two splake. On beige-and-chartreuse Cleos. Hans netted like a madman, two fish at a time. And a stiff, deep, clumsy but joyous tiff with a laker for me. Boated. Released. Maybe five pounds. But I don't think I envied the Indians' right to keep him. There was heavy, singing pressure on the line. There were greased lightning runs that bored down into that steely autumn lake. The audience included Hans and Walt and the boys, an eagle, two gray gulls, and that gold and red and patchwork hill north of the Onion River. Hans and Walt, fishless hosts, were utterly overjoyed: sportsmen. All this made Walt's now too common words—"It doesn't get better than this"—as we finished off the big bird before the fire that night, utterly true. Goodbye. 'Til next time! And a hug from Matt at the bus.

Up North. Thoreau's "in Wildness is the preservation of the world" gets at it best. Not just words, but words and things, men and boys and muskies and oaks and the sun on the hill and the bay. Thinking *and* doing, with all of the senses. As Thomas Lyon puts it in his *This Incomparable Lande:*

He [Thoreau] was profoundly aware of the physical content of thought and language, conscious that even in the most cerebral human activities the wild played an essential part. It was, indeed, as every evidence demonstrated to Thoreau, a "great pulse" preserving the world.

March 1990

Perhaps *up North* is that same *edge,* that narrowing free space between clapboard and deep forest, rational machinery and raw chaos, which is left us. At times it might even be this attic, right now echoing with the two warm notes of the mating chickadees—so different from their metallic Martian "dee-dee-dee"—and resounding mornings with the rasping wooden racketing of sandhill cranes, penetrating clapboards and my wooden head. *Up North* might just be always with us, available to imagination when frequently resorted to in the flesh.

Listen to the Quiet

On the Saturday before Thanksgiving, at 6 a.m., I have been in a deer stand listening to the quiet. For almost fifty years, now. For me, and many like me, it is the one fixed, still moment in a noisy year. What does the quiet say?

To begin with, silence tells me that I have finished the crashing and snorting of my unaccustomed walk in before-dawn woods. My awkward wriggling in the narrow tree stand of four-by-sixes has ended. The sharp "snap" of the shotgun action on a live round has put period to my fuss. Now I am ready to let the wooded eighty speak. The dark of an overcast November day, at six, narrows my senses down to hearing.

The quiet bothers me. Otherwise, my life is full of radio, TV, motor, voice noise. I bring noise with me to the woods. The woods responds with silence. I am programmed for aural signals. The woods is still. Maybe I'm so noisy here because the hush intimidates me. But that quiet is saying something. It says first: fear.

Once, in a pit blind above a rushy slough full of blackbirds I waited for mallards. I couldn't hear myself think for the racket of those redwings. Then, like a knife, quiet spoke. I caught the sharp cross of a marsh hawk's shadow on the Reed's canary grass. The blackbirds' quiet said: fear. The woods' quiet says it now. Fear of me.

Gradually, during the half hour 'til light, now, I hear a small wind in the poplar tips of my tree, the careen of a red squirrel on shagbark, the computer "dee-dee-dee" of a chickadee, even the faint click of small nails when the bird alights on my gun barrel. My quiet, as I gradually relearn it, lets the woods speak.

Of course I am listening for the big buck, the hoary swamp baron with the knobby, mossy, many spikes that will crown my career. I have been listening for him for nearly fifty years, not counting the time before I was old enough to hunt. It occurs to me that I will miss this silence, this waiting, after the greedy "crack" of the twenty drops him. Can any buck, elk, or hairy mammoth, reeking of rut and wilderness, finally answer my waiting quiet?

The deer that came, this year, was a glossy, squarish, Robin Hood sort of rogue, with four-inch spikes and an amused eye. Though I had heard eleven does a hundred yards away, I did not hear him 'til his eye caught mine. He was fifteen feet down and fifteen feet away in the deer trail that runs under that stand. He craned up, in silence, a long time—days, weeks?—then trotted a few steps behind another poplar to pick at brown, frozen fern. Thirty feet. I slip the safety, aim down at the slight hump between his shoulders . . . and miss. I forgot the lesson I have bored into every hunter I know: hold low when you shoot down.

My Sherwood Forest feast turned a neat half-circle around my tree, still at thirty feet but kind of quick, and poof! was gone. Now I had to learn to listen to a different quiet.

Dennis, my old friend and host here, a hundred yards away in his dead elm snag, had seen my buck. Now he said, low but clear, "You only missed *one*." "Of course I only missed one, how many *could* I have missed?" I thought. But this farmer lives nearer the woods than I do, and he speaks quietly too. With Dennis, I have to hear what's *not* said. What did *his* quiet mean? I figure it out—slowly.

The farmer's father Ray, from Jump River, spoke quiet too. He used to say that when you shoot a doe in November you kill three deer. Does usually drop twins in April or May. Sixty years ago, up North, the deer were few. Ray didn't shoot does. Now, fifty years later, the many deer feed on forty to eighty acres of Ray's son's corn. Several thousand dollars' worth. That's tough to take when the tractor loan sits at 11 percent. I had a Hunter's Choice permit. Dennis's quiet said, "Shoot a doe." Dennis never curses, but his quiet is more thunderous than expletives.

I sat still again, then, and felt failure, but also relief. My overshooting had pleased Dennis, and when I thought about it, had maybe pleased the spike, too. I felt a fool, but I sat, and the quiet of late dawn came back. A partridge materialized, as they tend to do, pecking at withered wild grape in the fence line. He froze as the high "KEEE!" of a redtail floated across the woods. Then, in a moment, rambled on to the next vine-wrapped cedar post. The chickadee came back with his brother and did a duet learned from some space alien, that same metallic "dee-dee-dee." My blood began to pulse to the same beat. I was, just then, transformed from a mobile, man-sized mousetrap, tensely pursuing meat, to a relative of the chickadee. I felt welcome here, no longer a hasty intruder. A shaft of bright sun began to warm my cold hands, then my back, and I sank happily into a gradually deepening doze. The hairy mammoth could go on

lurking in the swamp another twenty-five years if I had the luck to wait
for him like this. The woods felt like home.

November 1985

Deer may be stalked only for a single nine-day period once a year, unless
one is a bow-hunter. Their season is, of course, a major peak in the graph
of the year's retail sales. For many "hunters" this is the only edge time
experienced. Wisconsin schools accept deer hunting as an excuse for absence. For Dennis, though it is an important way to protect at least some
of the corn crop, it is mainly an old family tradition from Jump River, up
North.

Jakes

.

Webster gives "greenhorn; rube" as well as "a privy" (for the plural) when defining the word "jake." He does not give "immature male turkey," though that's how the word is used in Ferryville, in my cousin Jim's cabin on the Mississippi. That's how "jake" will be used here too, with maybe occasional whiffs of greenhorn and privy.

We drove to hunt the turkeys in spring, lucky recipients of permits for the May 5–9 slot. We hit the Kickapoo near dusk, drove up into public hunting land of five-hundred-foot ridges in the shape of a star with a small parking lot gouged out in the middle. Checking out some woody edges along an alfalfa field, we saw what we thought were ravens at a distance. Until they ran like deer, gobbled, and whumped off into the oak woods. Turkeys sound like the Concorde compared with the ruffed grouse that we traded to Missouri for them. Turkeys do live in Wisconsin, just like us.

Just like us. At the cabin, eight jakes and an old fart were preparing for the morning hunt. That is, at 9 p.m. when we got in the air was filled with beery snores and other exhalations. Kind of like a cabin I knew one November near Hurley, but a mite sharper that smell of used socks and scorched frying pans. No frost. Being as it was only the second day of the hunt, the bone piles in the corners were small. The aluminum scrap pile, though, was awesome, as they say in the East.

Dennis and I (as opposed to me and Joe) heaved ourselves up out of the cozy sacks at 3 a.m. and headed for the Kickapoo, forty-five minutes away over a few limestone ridges. He drove and I tried to keep him on course with a set of Geological Survey maps. The hill roads seemed regularly to make sudden lefts or rights just as you topped a forty-degree rise. We found the star-shaped ridge system again — maybe it's more like a bear paw — parked, loaded, and picked a ridgetop trail that seemed to point in the direction of yesterday's "ravens." My old buddy carried a rubberband-driven percussion yelper. I planned to bushwhack the gobblers as they flocked to his inspired notes.

It is a handsome site. Stars, whippoorwills, morning mist billowing up out of the curving river valley, and then, from every ridge end as it seemed, the various high or deep "gibble-ibble-ibble" calls as old farts an-

121

nounced their names and territories. Six points to the star—six gobblers declaring their intentions—then three more from across the river, from the ends of ridges that meshed with our bear paw like a cogwheel, the river supplying the lubricant. In the early light the whole scene seemed to move to the deep music of "Ubble-ubble-ubble."

Dennis, knowing my hunting prowess, simply stuffed me under a dry stump, sat on the cut end, and began to work the caller, not too loudly, once in twenty minutes. On the second day a heavy patter like a large child in the leaves betrayed a yard-tall black bird running uphill through last year's oak leavings. Coming toward our stump. The bird came well within the necessary twenty-five-yard range, but Dennis didn't know if it was the kind you might shoot. (We should have attended the state seminar.) Dennis can sex chickens, and even tell if they're good layers, but wild turkeys aren't partial to such familiarities. My buddy fidgeted, deep in thought, I flexed a small right toe muscle under the stump, and the big bird evaporated, gliding downhill at thirty-five per. At this point we were revealed as jakes: rubes.

During the spring season turkeys may be hunted only until noon. We headed back to Ferryville at twelve to ask the pros what we had seen. The pros told us (1) it might have been a hen and thus illegal, (2) hens have sky-blue heads, (3) hens seldom come to call when they're nesting, (4) hens have ghost-white heads, (5) it might have been a jake trying to sneak up on a mature gobbler's hen, (6) jakes have ghost-white heads, with a little red, (7) jakes have blue heads, (8) we might have seen a turkey buzzard attracted by our smell.

Our five days fell, generally, into these two halves: mornings we did our best to entice or sneak up on mating gobblers on the ridges, realizing that an engorged red head and wattles would reveal a bird as neither jake nor hen. From the conversation of the pros, between burps, we had gleaned that face paint or head netting, as well as camouflage clothing, is a must. Turkeys have eyes like eagles, though no particular sense of smell. We learned to move in the woods as if still hunting for deer—slowly, quietly, easing up to openings and over ridgetops. We tried to flit as ethereally as that first hen-jake-tom. As a bonus we got close-up views of pileated woodpeckers, American egrets by the river, and drumming grouse, whose rhythm set the atmosphere of every hunting morning. The quality of the hunt certainly seemed to be increased by the relatively small number of permit holders. We had five mornings of being in deep woods alone and it seems to us reasonable to wait even five years for another such experience.

While my cousin Jim and the other toms disappeared for their afternoon strut, Dennis and I, who thought of ourselves as top gobblers but reacted to the unexpectedly sharp relief of the ridge country like old farts, parked ourselves on the porch with Alfred to trade lies, watch the barges negotiate the Iowa side, and listen to the ballgame. I may have tasted an occasional ale. Dennis is a serious R.C. cola man. The habits of the ridge gobblers and the cabin gobblers were not, really, all that different.

Mature gobblers on the Kickapoo ridges slide down out of high oaks to strut and shout mornings and work their way downhill to water afternoons. The cabin gobblers crawled out to meet the ridge birds mornings and then slid downhill to watering spots on the Great River Road afternoons. The ridge gobblers strutted like drum majors in full display, tail feathers fanned, beards waving, heads and wattles a pulsing red. Cabin gobblers, in full display, sported clean T-shirts and fresh shaves—which turned *their* wattles red. They chose bar stools as the turkeys choose ridge ends, handy to the hens. The ridge hens seemed to be nesting, though, while the bar hens told our buddies to bug off.

The end of the five-day hunting period brought action, of a sort. Four of the cabin gobblers, two of them after missed shots at the less-than-fist-sized heads of tom turkeys, managed to wait until their called-up birds approached within twenty-five yards—which often means holding a motionless bead on your gobbler for what seems like hours—and hung up decent birds. Bragging later, they told how an enraged tom defending his turf would make the limestone ridge shake—not very likely, we thought.

But . . . on our second-last day Dennis and I, magnum sixes set for slaughter, waited fifteen minutes—it seemed a day at least—for a tom to come out from behind a dogwood, only to meet a red squirrel. The ground wasn't shaking, but we were. Then, when my buddy edged up to peek into a good-sized alfalfa field, having monitored "ibbles" from roughly that direction, and came upon a gobbler in full display—then we believed the pros' stories of "gobbler fever."

The tom, hearing the careful shuffle of Dennis's boots in the leaves of the logging road, apparently thought him a hen and approached, wattles engorged and tail fully fanned. Dennis, programmed to aim for the head, found this difficult because the display stance lowers the head against the breast and a breast full of sixes is no lunch at all. Hoping to perform a prefrontal lobotomy he zeroed in on the crown of the skull, fired, and the turkey sailed straight up and down like a bottle rocket. I loped across to cover the acre patch of hazel brush fifty yards away where the turkey seemed to have come down. Dennis ruefully catalogued the new cutover where his sixes had razed a dozen field-edge popples, invisible to him when he swung on the strutting tom. As Dennis came over to the hazel patch the tom lifted off thirty feet from me, gobbling, like the largest partridge ever. He seemed to have no trouble evading my tried-and-true six-years-too-late goose shot. Then Dennis and I kind of looked at each other for a while. Such a large bird leaves an awful quiet when he goes.

When we got back to Ferryville with our story there was a twenty-five-pound gobbler hanging in the fish-cleaning shack and the assembled cabin toms had already descended on the helpless Father of Waters. When they returned, shaking their wattles, we hardly had the spirit to tell them of our miss.

Dennis and I, now feeling ourselves to be both bonafide jakes and old farts, slunk off the next morning after purloining a wing-feather each for our sons at home. We spent a last hour on the star-shaped ridge, heard again the challenging "ibbles" and "ubbles" and the one-lunger John Deere roar of ruffed grouse wings. We were, we found, utterly pleased that turkeys are loose in Wisconsin again, that it's possible, even on an occasional permit, to play pilgrim father on the Kickapoo. We'll gladly wait our turn to be jaked again, but we hope to be back in some not too distant May to feel the ground shake.

August 1988

Like "Up North" and the piece that follows, this one entails an excursion outside Waupaca County to hunt — and to ruminate. Such excursions give me, or Dennis and me, a chance to compare our management of Bear Creek township with the larger Wisconsin scene. Bluffs and the Mississippi are certainly awe-inspiring, and pretty well kept up, but the governor could still take a lesson from the Bear Creek area, if only in the matters of political savvy, simple charm, and humility.

A Good Way to Miss a Turkey

This spring we went east of Seneca on the high ridges over the Mississippi, to hunt turkeys again. We took camouflage, cushions, decoys, deodorant, and even a shotgun. We tried hard. We got skunked. And it was a good hunt. Here's how.

We are quietly descending a hill road—a forty-five-degree logging trail—on Albert Roberts's farm. We hope to deceive the Wisconsin variant of *Meleagris gallopavo,* but our resonant stumbling down the loose limestone, fallen oak branches, and splashy mud which *are* the road defeats us. Some dozen turkeys are startled into early flight. They buzz as if slung from catapults out of the fifty-foot oaks which are their roosts. They curse and "ibble" as they arc across the deep valley. We give up our surprise attack and go back to the top of the ridge to regroup. It is still just 5:30, first light.

Our further campaign involved setting a decoy in a corner of Albert's hilltop pasture, fading behind a brush pile in the adjacent ridgeside woods, and calling the turkeys to us. The birds seem to fly to the ridge tops mornings and then to gobble, feed on acorns, and mate on their way down to the valley cornfields. Fifty yards from a wide gap in the pasture fence—they don't, generally, like to cross fences—we subsided into last year's leaves. When distant dawn "ibbles" and "obbles" set in, Dennis replied sparingly with the slightest of "skrep-skrep" invitations, scribed on a slate disc. Maybe once in half an hour. Seemingly, a turkey whisper. Dennis conceals even the slight movement of his hands on the slate. Turkeys appear, at times, to be all sharp eye. For a long time nothing replied.

A pasture edge in first light, in April, has multiple charms and distractions, even before the leaves are out. The mad, sharp cry of mating wood ducks sounds from deep valley ponds. The romancing aria of the cardinal is particularly fine and melodious. It isn't difficult to lose your concentration.

Dennis "skrep"ed again, after what seemed to me a distant "ibble," but no heavy scurry was audible in the wet leaves. I reduced my senses to sight alone and, bored with the view of a papier-mâché turkey hen, turned to catch the slight shudder of a large, pale oak leaf at the tip of my extended boot. No. Yes. The leaf was winter-bent in a double tunnel shape. Some-

thing tiny and pale, a nose, loomed small at one of the entrances. A creature the size of my little toe, the bright tan color of beech leaves, fast,
mounted the boot tip and withdrew. Returned, hesitated, buried itself under the leaf again. . . . A procession—four fox squirrels—awakened my
hearing as they passed from left to right in the woods behind us. Dennis
called once more, but I was waiting for the least shrew—for my toe-sized
visitor was that—to show again. I bent my head to see better, squinted at
the oak leaf, and WHOOSH sounded behind me in the pasture. Dennis, my
guide and caller, said, a touch dryly, "There went your gobbler."

Shame. Gloom. Hopelessness. The temptation to blame the whole thing
on a failed childhood, as usual. Maybe it's time to take up canasta?
    We waited a while longer. Hunting *is* open until noon. But we de-
cided, as Kenny Rogers says, that you gotta know when to fold 'em. We
started back for the car. It's been a cold spring in Wisconsin. The gobblers
weren't really breeding until the next, warmer week. We missed a heavy
spring blizzard by heading home early, birdless as we were. But why, how
could I call this a good hunt?

I am sitting today, a week after Seneca, on the river bank behind the
small college where I teach and learn. I'm not packing a double twelve this
time, but I am—I think—hunting. I am trailing a slight thing, a thought
as pale and elusive as that least shrew that saved my giant tom turkey's
life. Here, behind the chemistry department, I am trying to distill the
smoky essence of the chase. Since I'm at college, I start with a very present college thought. Political correctness.
    My township, Bear Creek, is as rurally remote as it sounds, but when
a dairyman member of the school board referred to "the creeping cancer
of political correctness" at last Monday's meeting, everyone caught the reference. We are, in Bear Creek, generally hairy, aware, and opposed to new
(or used) doctrine. Just because it *is* doctrine.
    Animal rights, then. I hunt deer and, mostly, ruffed grouse. I clean
and eat the game when I've been lucky or, even, skillful. I have in the recent past chased and killed the teddy-bear raccoon for his hide and for
the toothsome barbecue he makes. I do these things because boys and
men, in Genesee where I grew up, did them. Fifty years ago.
    Now I think of last week's hunt with Dennis, of the shame of the lost
concentration, the lunk-headed distraction, that deprived me of a shot at
a gobbler. My lunk-headedness doesn't, now, much disturb me. But this
means that we drove five hundred miles, spent three hundred dollars, ago-
nized through the spring blizzard that delayed us, lugged our gear down
a muddy hill road and called in a wily tom in order *not to shoot.* As I think

this, two first-run, half-grown spring rabbits are cropping the begin-
nings of turf six feet from me. Mourning doves, hotly pursued game in
Arizona but protected here, are "oooaaa"ing up a rainstorm. A gray squirrel with a ratty, shedding tail is failing to find last fall's hidden provisions
and muttering darkly about it. I haven't the least desire, just now, to
shoot and eat these creatures. Why not? Because people—you too—are
various at various times, I think, and not easily pigeon-holed.

The difficulty with political correctness, about animal rights, or gen-
der, or race, or even sexual preference, is that it must be intolerant in its
defense of a single principle. This is true, I think, because history is per-
ceived as a record of mere oppression. The knee-jerk reaction to mere oppression is inflexible righteousness. For some reason, though, inflexible
righteousness doesn't work. Why not?

Let's take the matter of hunting and animal rights. That is, after all,
the atmosphere of this sermon. For the advocate of animal rights, the taking of animal life is absolutely wrong. I, on the other hand, think that human beings are predators and that predation will continue to be a human
activity, whether open or hidden, hunting and/or aggressively attempting
to increase one's returns on the "free" market. But I don't think that we are
only predators. I think that our humanity consists, in no small measure,
in the ability to enjoy something beyond simple consumption.

As Dennis and I trotted down that rocky, greasy hill road, a barred owl
called, and the rush of flung turkeys gobbled and ibbled enormously. The
whole stable of woodpeckers, from downy to hairy to pileated, punctuated
the between-ridge stillness with distinctly various rats and tats. The dawn
drumrolls of ruffed grouse, that almost motor thumping that has been rare
at this low point of the grouse cycle, rub-a-dubbed clear and loud in the
April air. The eighteen-wheelers that tend to drown out such sounds in our
Green Bay area flats seldom attempt the ridge roads. The distant hoots of
barge tows and trains going along the Mississippi, however, seemed—in
their remoteness—an organic part of the sound world of hunting, too. Taking these sounds home with me, I have not diminished them, but rather
amplified them. And, as it happens, though my intentions were bloody (I
would say, quite normally so) my "bag" on this hunt was both rich, and various, and quite immaterial. I do not think that I am an unusual hunter in
this respect. Dennis, and a whole host of hunting companions past, have
happily collected cardinal song without too much concern for the certainty
of turkey fricassee. I certainly hunted in a more stressed way when I was
younger. But no one stays young forever.

Dennis, for example—a last one, I promise—has reached the ad-
vanced age of forty-four. He hunts deer with the rifle and the bow. He seldom misses with the rifle. He has yet to kill with the bow, though he

shoots just as well with it. His wife Deb, noting the time and effort expended on bow hunting, asked him about this apparent lapse in slaughter. "Well" he said, "the rifle deer go by quickly, and they drop or they don't. Bow hunting you see the deer for a while, get to know him and look into his eyes, so to say. By the time he's in range, he's a friend. I don't feel like shooting, then."

St. Hubertus, patron of hunters, is said to have met a buck with a crucifix between its horns while hunting on Good Friday. In this way he became a Christian. Maybe, meeting animals as hunters do, they, also, one by one, are "converted." Not to the religion of veggie-burgers, but to beauty, kinship, even love for the hunted. It might even be that hunters love their quarry more than the politically correct defenders of the same. Maybe gradual association works better than righteousness, all across the board.

May 1993

As this hunting calendar, edge biography nears its conclusion, I find that I've become longer on thought, association, even—dammit—doctrine. Is this the result of age, experience, or an old head wound? More likely, I fear, a desire to preach learned all too thoroughly in a hundred classrooms where no one dared to interrupt me. I am, however, aware of the difference between my views and Truth, and of the rapidity with which my final full-stop is approaching. Why, that's enough to make a fellah *think*.

Foxes and Men

These days I spend a good deal of down time—off season, non-hunting time—examining the nature of the pleasure and pain I encounter hunting ruffed grouse. Every newspaper and magazine, Hell, every Rice Krispies box, tells me that I am a savage, a sadist, a misbegotten monster when I try to kill birds. Several good woodsmen that I used to know have given it up, given in, spend their Saturdays watching TV with the rest, or maybe playing Bingo, for all I know. Even my wife's attitude has become rather frosty. Hadn't I, really now, better hang it up?

Trying to kill ruffed grouse. It's that first word, "trying," that maybe keeps me from trading the old worn-silver Browning twenty over/under for a good television set and a quarter-barrel of Miller Lite. Just *trying*. Never coming to the end of the popple coverts, of tense, weathered old men, of the critical and loving eyes of springers and Brittanies and English setters. Never tiring of that last flick sideways and up behind the black ash or white spruce that saves the smallish bird—though it always seems pretty big. And then, the smell of potato chips and dip will never replace powder reek, blowing the smoke out of both barrels, cursing softly with short, pungent words.

The frost on the breeze in the morning is another good thing. I've opened the back door, twenty gauge in my left; Pete's in the yard with the two yipping Brittanies, Tracey and Nettie B. We are all about to depart the world of readymade, off-the-shelf, post-Thanksgiving Day sale life. This time is ours to do and make. "The Mack?" "O.K.!" Then we're coasting at forty, watching the sky for tundra swans, inhaling the big thermos of coffee ahead of time, and talking birds.

Mostly, the talk is of sudden drops into muddy slough holes, grouse raised as you climb carefully through prickly ash or blackberry canes, friend Mike *throwing* his double—just once, at the railroad tracks that the escaped russet bird had crossed safely above two and a quarter ounces of eights. Friend Mike is no hothead. It was just that a perfect string of misses had gotten *to* him that sunny yellow-beige day at the Mack. Hasn't at least the thought of ending one's obvious incompetence with the miserable, satisfying CRACK! of walnut against steel ever occurred to you? (The gun landed—maybe on purpose—in a pillow of

Reed's canary grass. It was, of course, quite empty, though hot.) The talk, then, is about trying and often failing.

At the Mack—a public hunting ground—Pete parks the old, red van in a clearing next to those very tracks. As the wind is soft and southerly, the sun hazy at 9:30, we follow Tracey and Nettie B. south on a cross-country ski trail just dusted with new snow. Crows hail us and flap off east: There's a gut pile from last week's deer season surrounded by the black ones' narrow tracks. There's also an earlier set of neat fox feet staps from last night. Our brother predators have been here earlier. Licensed hunters aren't the only carnivores afield and hungry.

The trail winds through slough grass, misses the alder copses that tangle skis, angles southwest. After a quarter-mile, with the railroad tracks and the van out of sight, we give up on finding trail edge birds and begin to visit the copses that are now closer together, preparing to form serious brush. Partridge berries hang red near the snow and there are, after a while, three-toed tracks showing a fine fringe of grouse snowshoe netting. The tracks amble gently from bush to bush. One, two, several sets. "Roost near here," says Pete, and Tracey and Nettie begin to hum with their tails. Good tune.

Where the alder and popple gets thicker—where I have to edge side-ways to pass and the brush is a good yard above head height—Tracey points, circles, and disappears. Then her steel bell falls still. "Point?!" asks Pete, and "thrum-whoosh!" comes his invisible answer. The dogs have found a—"thrum-whoosh, whooosh, whoosh"—no, a whole pod of grouse. After the long fall the birds have gathered together where the feed is, or maybe just for company. The tinkling bells say that the pod has— "thrum"—mostly gone south.

A hundred yards ahead Nettie stands pointing in an open swale— foxtail and canary grass—and I heed Pete's "Move, dammit! Keep up with her!" As I pass Nettie, who is stiff as a poker, a gray grouse hums against alder, swings back in my face, passes a foot above the blaze orange stocking cap that is generally swinging from a prickly ash but just then is on my head. I turn—professional for once—to take the grouse going away, then hastily drop the barrels as Pete, forty yards behind me, ducks to let the buzzing turkey?—no, just a twelve-ounce grouse—pass *him*. "Bu-Bang!" but a shower of fine alder kindling is the only result. "Too blessed *soon!*" Pete, by far the better shot, has this once been startled into hasty action. There are, still, three birds somewhere ahead.

Nevertheless, we stop a moment, share an apple—a Wolf River and large—and smoke a cigarette. This hunting is, then, not only utterly un-PC but also deadly, mortal. That might be part of the charm. Pete thanks me, curtly but warmly, for dropping the barrels, for not ventilating the gray thatch. "It wasn't hard. I didn't need to drag your carcass to the road through that popple." "Lazy ass, as usual," says jovial Pete.

This day the birds won't rise above the Wisconsin brush. Pete and I, and maybe even the wearying Brittanies, for once envy New England grouse hunters, habitués of more open coverts or of neglected apple orchards. Even a good, long lunch break on a high bank of a wide, ash-lined ditch in Monet light doesn't restore what the close-set alder and raspberry canes have taken. (Thirty years of this brush-busting have taken something too.) When a further hour of snow reading, confused by afternoon overcast and a now fickle wind, brings us back on our own morning tracks, we decide to hang it up for that day. I follow the trail we've made and find a pair of Pete's empties—yellow twenties. Pete is aggressively anti-litter and reloads his own shells besides. It's pretty clear that that moment when I might have perforated the gray head had *impressed* my old shooting buddy. I announce this find to Pete, who is fifty yards east and on a parallel track. The answer: "Look out for that buzz-bomb bird, then, after a hundred yards or so." Pete is still hunting, worn out or not.

In a hundred yards, though, we are out of the alder jungle altogether, a bit to the west of our entry point, and by some trick of landscape, or maybe even doubtful woodcraft, we can see the van barely four hundred yards away. Young Nettie, who has had enough, is frankly following Pete's footsteps. Tracey seems to be resting her gray nose on a fallen branch in the midst of the wide-open birch grove that frames the not-so-distant van. Waiting for us to catch up? *Pointing!*

As Pete and I and Nettie straggle rather hurriedly through the birch grove, Tracey shifts and freezes on a small tuft of foxtail. Forty yards before us *our* ruffed grouse breaks cover, saluted by "Bu-Bang!," this time one "Bang!" each. Followed by an immediate bass duet of "Yours!" Tracey, as is meet, returns the bird to her master. There is, though, nothing for it but to share the day's one bird.

A good, long minute is spent admiring the glossy, green-black ruff, reading futures in the sharp, though glazing, eye. Quiet angel moment. Fox tracks thread this birch grove too, like the ski trail this morning. They bring to mind now, for both hunters at once—though hardly for the dogs who are fox-like and presumably live in *this* moment—Winslow Homer's glorious painting, *The Fox Hunt.* There the red one, Reynard, realizes that the sea is in his path as ravenous crows mob him to his death. This hunter, and, doubtless, Pete, can foresee in the ruffed grouse's eye, in the painting suggested by fox tracks and the morning's fox and crows, a not dissimilar end. Football, TV, off-the-shelf life doesn't grant *this* vision. Hunters, who kill their own meat, know their mortal place in the world. That's the real "big picture." That's the bottom line.

No, I won't hang up the twenty just yet. I'm barely beginning to understand this life.

March 1996

Perhaps you, like my friend Jim, think I am a bit paranoid here. I can only say that hunters do catch a good deal of flack these days. And maybe you too appreciate a good football game on TV. I tried to write not *against* TV and potato chips but *for* a more active, less consumption-oriented life. Through writing about hunting, I have discovered the emotional—not theoretical—recognition of mortality which it can teach those who are willing to learn. This seemed, and seems, a useful lesson.

Connections

"THUNK!" At 6:10 a.m. on an overcast October day there had only been a live red flash before impact. Nathan, the neighbor with whom I ride to work, had no time to brake or swerve. That flash had to have been a red fox. A quarter-hour later my neighbor said, "He won't try that again." With Nathan, that's a month's conversation.

This piece is about the impact of civilization on nature at that edge where the two meet, in the woods and in us. Nathan, no sadist, will wait forever for two hen mallards to disentangle their broods and waddle away from the white center line. The fox had taken him utterly by surprise; foxes are generally more careful. What my neighbor said, "He won't try that again," was good science, even good philosophy, not just smart talk. Generally speaking, you only get one chance on the edge. Neither civilization nor nature are, in themselves, forgiving. The Ford poisoned our air and we are poisoned. The fox misjudged velocity, his or ours, and died.

I learn things on this morning edge, early and in the dark, for after fifty years of hunting the edge has come, it seems, to follow me. Just as the roads where foxes die, or make it across, run everywhere, so too the fox's edge runs everywhere beside the roads, offering single chances. When Nathan dropped me where our daily work paths split, on Ballard Road, I had two miles of city streets to walk, but also two miles of edge to watch. This is especially true at 6:45, for it is dark, quiet, and early enough for the streets still to be deserted. It is a time for edge creatures.

The sun begins to rise. Crows—*Corvus brachyrhynchos*—on highlines stretch one wing and then the other. They look like leftover rags of midnight, and sound like that too. Then the subliminal clicks of increasing light send them in search of carrion even riper than I am. I start walking.

Two blocks further, turning southwest, there is a length of narrow meadow bordered, on the street side, with alternating ashes and maples. Late in October these are as sumptuous as Handel's *Water Music.* I march beneath them, as luxurious in deep scarlet, bronze, and gold as Harun al-Rashid in *Arabian Nights.* Then the tracks on the far side of this meadow ring with locomotive music, so rare and archaic now that the deep brassy baying sounds natural, of nature. The engine's moan echoed on the rail-

133

road edges of youth which led lonely and cross-country to rich stands of asparagus and trestles for skinny-dipping divers and old men fishing bull-heads. My Baghdad palace of leaves is not dispersed by this blast, but en-riched. The Water Music gains a deeper note.

Appleton, a paper mill town, is still rich in unpulped trees. Elms un-til twenty-five years ago, oak and maple and ash now, with a good admix-ture of willow, honey locust, mountain ash, and conifers. The blue spruce at the end of Haroun's parade is full of redstart, so much life can one quick spark of bird impart to dark boughs. The house behind, white clapboard, of course, fades against the quick snip-snap of the hungry beak, feasting even this late on the last mosquitoes. Then I cross the still echoing tracks — well after the train, I'm no fox — and cut south under mostly maple and white oak, this last, again, the kind with rounded points on the palmate leaves. Here I pass a small door in a red brick wall and recall my twenty-five-year-old divorce. This used to be the marriage counselor's office. The memory, no longer bitter, is utterly final. "He won't try that again."

Next an angle across a factory parking lot — I walk the hypotenuse when it's available — and the view of a miniature prairie: foxtail, black-eyed susans, marsh daisies, columbine. Someone has thoroughly planted that strip between the sidewalk and street usually left to frowsy Kentucky blue-grass. A nice, rough contrast with the mundane brown stubble left by the frost in the other yards. *This* urbanite is edgy, free.

Around the next corner there's a mountain ash loaded with carmine, flat berries. No customers just yet, though. About this time last year a flock of cedar waxwings made this tree vibrate with harvest and greed and beauty. Those birds may be heading our way right this minute. The wind, a mild norther, is right for them. I'm almost tempted to wait, think I can feel their approach. Their bright tan and yellow, black and white, and their pointed hoods, lit and warmed several good days last fall. Time to get on to the office, though.

The next two furlongs, straight and due south, run beneath big trees amputated and odd for the sake of telephone wires. This stretch is, fur-ther, redolent of smoked ham and sausage. Jacob's Market, which used to cut up deer in season and still makes venison sausage if you bring in the boned meat, is right here. Most of the old butchers, like barbers, were hunters and fishermen. Blood sport somehow goes with those two trades. The edge runs right through Jacob's, gets trimmed with the suet.

There is, I gradually realize, no urban enclave, no Florence flask com-pletely sealed away from edge, from the reciprocal chafing and feeding of polity and wildness. This process goes on everywhere. The white clap-board of the houses, the tensile steel of Nathan's Ford, come also from the earth. How to understand the ubiquitous interaction of civil and wild?

First, neither polis nor forest can *care*, finally. Both are organized for general survival, unmoved by particular death. When I prefer the edge, the place where the two realms rub, I choose to recognize nature's naked acceptance of accident, change, and mortality as opposed to society's impossible though unconscious promise of enduring order and safety. The cement upon which I pace here in town only *seems* eternal compared with Harun al-Rashid's leafy Turkish fabrics: the autumn maples and ashes. All rush to oblivion, as do I. How can one bear it?

Well, this quarter-mile ends at the campus where I teach and learn. There, today, a hundred yards beyond a white oak which supports seventeen fat gray squirrels, is another mountain ash, called *ryabina* in Russian. Right now this tree is filled with the flutter and gulp of what must surely be "my" flock of waxwings. They've come for berries redder than this morning's fox. The birds and the tree, the lover and his lass, but also the hunter and his prey, even the Ford and the fox, are vitally close, made of the same particles and for each other. They exchange life and death and produce, together, the benign indifference which is also a living closeness—the groundswell of all being. Our particular shapes do rush toward oblivion, but maybe neighbor Nathan was not utterly right. In further forms, in later guises, the matter that is us, the living particles, do resurrect, "try that again." The fox, the Ford, and you and I are—then—all together immortal.

January 1996

Here, for once, I've taken you to town. I go often enough to buy salt and shotshells and, well, to make a living teaching at my small college, called Lawrence University by way of sounding cosmopolitan. Even on these journeys, though, I find myself on the edge, making connections, very much alive. In *town*—fancy that!

Hunting the Edges

Leaving the clapboard farmhouse, turning my back on the white paint, going hunting. Alone, as no one's around just now. The snap of the double's breech on sixes accentuates the sharp north breeze. Might be a pheasant in Rohan's corn edge, tracks in the snow. On the way to the south side of the little woods. Off we go.

We? No dogs after Pyos. Memory. Today, just the memory of Pete and *his* dogs: Teague, Teague II, Trace, and now Nettie B. I apprenticed to Pete as a partridge hunter, after a lapse of college, city years. Thirty years ago.

We were talking about hunting, then, in the faculty lounge. It beats talking investments and somehow you seldom talk about your "field." Maybe because our fields all have different vocabularies. Maybe because field becomes *must* work, hunting is *choice.* Anyway, Mojmir, displaced Czech, remembered birds snared at the fences of the Esterhazy estate near Brno. Brother Bogdan had gapped those fences to make a path for the gaudy birds, a path to the pot. Did we ever see pheasants here? Pete and I both heard, came up with a pheasant each. A bottle of Mojmir's mother's homemade slivovitz was our reward. ("Do you like it, slivovitza?" "Huh!" After slivovitz you exhale.) Mainly, though, Mojmir's glowing smile, visible return to youth, village, estate fences. Memory of brother, mother, and the physical self-sufficiency — always partial — of home near Brno. Memory too of poaching, living on the legal edge, which was, is, perforce, the only hunting of many men in crowded Europe. Those who care to hunt, to cultivate some partial self-sufficiency. Not so many, any more. Here either.

And here's the oak copse, fallen trunk, brown oak leaves — round at the ends: white oak — on snow. Here Pyos once caught a falling grouse like a ball. Stone dead in the air. Pete's tutoring.

Pete did his teething on his mother's Parker double in North Dakota. Ducks. Teaching in Wisconsin, in a duck-poor place and time, he soon picked up ruffed grouse shooting. Had a big half-collie, half-Brittany. Teague. Took me with, after the slivovitz. It was, I think, a year before I could see the grouse go in the noisy dust of the takeoff, two before the barrels pointed anywhere near right. (I'm not naturally centered or quick, as you ought to have gathered by now.)

It was the thirteenth year of a marriage that, for all its promise, was a mismatch. My fault too. Couldn't learn to say "Yes," "No." Silently turned a critical eye. And then there was no marriage, no white paint. There was Pete, and the wood's edge, but no clapboard to bring the game to. I hadn't known how important that was, that return to the white paint.

Anyway, as the paint was flaking off we drove north for grouse and deer. The journey was long and late and well lubricated. We stopped at every little tap for billiards and beer. A fellow hunter, bewailing a missed opportunity with snow geese, babbled of "a snock of flows." A couple of stops later I knew exactly what he meant. By morning, in Pete's cabin, I was elevated to that common point where I easily raveled out all the checks, false scents, and whole missed trail of my imminent divorce, then made everyone involved happy. Canadian Seven Crown can do that. But sooner or later the blue velvet falls from your eyes.

That day, wandering the curvy line of a popple edge, vacant and puzzled, I let my mouse-trap muscles free to follow a sprung red grouse, saw it shudder and hump. When I couldn't find it I fetched Teague and Pete to my knife, stuck in a tree on the bird's line. Teague pulled the bird from a rabbit hole in a sandy pocket. My first. And though there was no place to go with it, it marked a step toward . . . mastery? That's what I thought then. No, I was competing—hopelessly—with Pete's mastery. Wanting to be praised, in a world suddenly vacant. I couldn't get that white paint out of my mind, or accept it wholly, either.

The partridge hunt was a prelude. Deer season opened that Saturday. Besides Pete and me, Charles, farmer turned pilot when the milk prices dropped, rolled in. That same Charles of the palmate buck horns. When I think about it now, Charles just underlined the general edginess of my life. Pete is an English professor, a colleague in my professional life. Charles, buddy and hunting companion since high school, was, for me (Charles despises symbolism), a representative of my past, farm, "real" life. I expect that I wanted this deer hunt to paste together a life made questionable by divorce. (This *was* a while ago, when both theory *and* divorce seemed significant.)

We were hunting west of Riley Lake in an east wind and on a gray day. We had hunted ruffed grouse here enough to know a few trails, to have seen at least one decent eight-point buck. Charles and Pete, no tyros, took stands near the crossings of narrow, well-used trails. Restless, I chose to still hunt, in my case a fancy phrase for wandering around. I did keep their locations in mind, the directions not to shoot, the trails, toward them, not to follow. I walked, marched, the main logging road from the car to Riley Lake, three miles each way. I knew, I hope, that I wasn't hunting, that my Mauser was, indeed, surplus.

About even with Charles and Pete, who posted south of me, was a tiny box-stall barn. In it a draft horse thumped, shifted its weight, snorted quietly. It was used to snaking logs out of the woods on every day but a deer season day, I expect. The horse's thumps and lunges in the little box barn made me aware of my larger ones. I drifted back toward the road. A shot. I stopped. For a moment—two minutes, ten?—I was hunting again, watching for movement, stilled against a shape-screening cedar, doing rather than self-pitying. Then I fell back into my restless dance, lit a Camel. Smoke blowing in my face, I started back toward the lake. Like an expectant *father*, damn it. And saw the buck.

In the middle of the logging road. Stopped in mid-stride. The cover of any November sporting journal. It dawned then: "that's what I'm here for," and, cigarette still glowing, I slipped the safety, raised the rifle, squeezed. I don't remember a bang. The buck continued north. A quick second shot, hurled pretty heedlessly, made the buck disappear. I walked to where he'd stood, seventy-five feet from me. Nothing. Five yards into the brush I found bright blood. Then a slight decline of stained alder leaves and the buck dead. One hole, back of the shoulder. And then I howled. *YEAH-haa!* Nashville style. Seven nice points and a lump. The lump was, is, too small to hang a hat on. (The warden who registered the deer gave him three years, by the teeth.) Calling up an *Outdoor Life* how-to piece, I wrestled the guts out, bagged the heart and liver. Sat down for another Camel. Pure adrenaline.

So far, so good. But now I needed applause. I crossed south to inform Pete and Charles—as if they hadn't heard. They were congratulatory, even though the buck had passed so close to Charles that he'd been afraid to raise his .30–30 and spook him, then shot fast and too late. The shot I'd heard. After a sufficiency of my babble they suggested, nicely, that they wanted to hunt too, that I might be better occupied dragging my buck out. I imagine that I expected a procession with drums and curly brass trumpets. I discovered, though, that dragging even my first buck on a corduroy road was a fairly quiet, wearing activity. Not much like a parade at all. I sulked.

That evening, the buck hung from the meat pole, it took two whiskeys for me to go for my rifle, celebratory salutes in mind, joy shots. Pete—bearded, genial, but serious—let me know that no gun would be touched in his cabin when the whiskey was going. I was hurt, went to my sleeping bag miffed: I was an ass.

The next day, in a heavy snow that turned into a blizzard, Charles and Pete tried to fill their tags, fight the weather, and — as I see it now — put up with my infantile behavior. I wanted to be praised; not for the buck which had fallen to the gun by sheer luck and at no great range. But praise for my *existence*, praise and respect, even love which, I think, I felt I had forfeited by choosing divorce. Charles and Pete, though, were — are — hunters, not shrinks. Wrapped in red wool blankets against the unusual blast of wind, they did their best to track another buck. As they read the sign they realized that their quarry was able both to elude them and to consummate a relationship with a doe that *he* was tracking. Charles, Pete, the buck, the doe were *doing*, doing what the wood's edge is for. I walked the Riley Lake road again, dragging my rifle, caught and clumping like the furloughed logging horse. It was, then, a relief to return south — even to emptiness — and dump the then meaningless buck at the butcher's.

That was twenty-four years ago. Right now, as I walk east, along Rohan's slough, the approach of a stand of red aspen reminds of a hunt *this* year with that same Peter. There have been, in between, a number of years when I hunted without him, or he without me; I'm not sure which. Age, the departure or imminent departure of offspring — what wildlife management calls "diffusion" — maybe even self-knowledge and appreciation of what I now take to be Pete's just complaints, have made hunting together possible, a pleasure again. This year we returned, after twenty years, to Deer Creek, a six-square-mile mosaic of willow and ash, tamarack and nine-foot aspen, open marsh and the canary grass edge of old logging trails and drainage ditches. We were hunting ruffed grouse.

Not much west wind, forty-degree weather, grouse- and woodcock-colored leaves under foot. Nettie B., the three-year-old Brittany and her mentor, old Trace. Trace is kind of deaf now, can't see too well, but a real professional: minimum, elegant tracking, no extra moves.

Deer Creek, like most of our local hunting grounds, is not big woods. There are only occasional ridges of hardwood tall enough to have shaded out the bird cover. The grouse, the deer, the snowshoe hares are found next to the ridges, between marsh and forest, or on forest edges that neighbor with cornfields. We hunt what the English used to call the marches, the boundaries — the edges. The meeting of field, or marsh, and forest provides a combination of browse and quick invisibility, that is, concentrations of game and openings where you have a chance to gun for it. Then, too, these edges provide, maybe, a relief from shelter, "a nipping and an eager air," distance from that white paint and civilization. Deer Creek is all "edge" this day.

It began slowly. Fifty yards apart, the dogs ahead into the small wind in popple that rimmed taller hardwood. The Brittanies soon run with the tautness that means bird scent, but a quarter-mile, one side of forty-acre square, yields no flushes. We come up onto a high-sided north–south ditch, cross to more popple edge, raise something — a woodcock, I say, from the flash of bright tan against gray popple, the absence of the partridge's "thrum-whoosh" — then a point from Trace and the just-mentioned roar after all. One ruffed grouse, at least, but it rocketed far out, across the main ditch, north and to Pete's right. We pursue the earlier bright tan clue, end with a point and a woodcock indeed. We are well started.

Successful hunters are quick bores. In perhaps an hour we have ten woodcock for twelve shots, a limit. Not too shabby for us fledgling geezers. If this seems greedy, I ought to say that for the two of us it's the second time in twenty years. We've blundered into the fall flight to Louisiana, we see another fifteen birds, we are warmed as if with peppermint schnapps. Two details: While Trace is a veteran, Nettie B., although three, has never pointed. In the course of this busy ramble she makes her first four points. Bravo, Nettie B.! And then, it's been some years since I hunted over dogs. My bag of game for a season has been, since my springer Pyos departed, like Faulkner's description of a poker hand: "a small pair, a very small pair." Today, for the first time in five years, the crack of the twenty was regularly followed by a burst of bright tan feathers. I felt almost as good as Nettie B.

There have been some drawbacks. Trace has done most of the finding, but has been lost several times when she couldn't hear Pete. I've lost my direction and come out on an unexpected piece of unknown ground, too. Still, we seem to be approaching a hunting mood which my son David would call "awesome."

Later we walked a mixed maple and ash ridge back toward the car. We're hoping still for grouse but inwardly convinced that we have, for once, really run up against the low point in the cycle. That first bird, flushing far ahead of us a second time, seemed simply to disappear. Ruffed grouse are famous for that. Now, on the ridge, we walk single file, keep an eye on the dogs, but don't honestly expect them to make game up here. Because we feel, with our limits of woodcock, that the hunt is over, we talk. Whoever happens to be walking in the lead tends to narrate — the one behind is the audience.

We're both a bit deaf, maybe from too many years of unprotected shooting—rather like old Trace. We can't, either of us, catch all of the words. Still, we pick up enough to know that we're still hunting with the same companion; the tone, the burden of the stories hasn't changed much. Hell, most of them are the same as twenty years ago, they've just sprouted gray whiskers, like us. "Remember when Dave shot . . .?" "Remember the time Mike lost . . .?" It's almost like the ancient joke about giving stories numbers. We don't catch the rest of the account, but we know it by heart: My brother-in-law Dave shot a decent buck in the head at seventy-five yards, with a shotgun, and killed it on the spot—then passed up a huge swamp-baron following the smaller buck because he thought shooting for the party, after he had one, piggish. You know that story. Mike, the historian, hunter, colleague at our small college, lost track of his English setter Klute, found him only after sunset beneath a tree with nine—counting the number of flushes—ruffed grouse in it. The tales are as worn as the wooden beads of a rosary. They all come, too, from this same edge. Not this Deer Creek edge, but that general edge where hunters thrive, not too close to viewless jungle to shoot, but not right up against the white paint either. In the short popple and tag alder, next to the open marsh and corn stubble.

We followed a neglected DNR ski trail and when the ridge sloped back down into marsh we walked beside canary grass and alder. When we looked about after the last tale Trace was vibrating "ruffed grouse," though she hadn't pointed yet. All eyes on Trace. She's working out the bird's feeding perambulations among the red partridge berries. Veterans like Trace, even if a bit deaf, know about where the bird should be. Just across this well-used deer trail . . . And we forget all about young Nettie B. Who is on point higher up the ridge. Quite visible and quite ignored, until the bird—bored—flashes silver gray straight out over open marsh and away.

There is nothing like the shared stupidity of professors, of hunting professors, to facilitate what idiots call a bonding experience. A good laugh, and a peppermint at the nearest tap—never all that far in Wisconsin—conclude that lesson and day. That's no small part of hunting the edges.

Warmed through by this last memory, I cut a corner of Rohan's slough to reach corn stubble and the direct route across the forty to the white clapboard house. "Whooosh! Thrrum!" A double of ruffed grouse—one red, one gray—floats out of the alders ahead of me, swings lazily—as they will when you're not really hunting—back into wild cucumber over an oak blowdown. "Enough," I feel. That's what enough feels like. "Enough" is what the edge has, finally, taught me.

January 1995

"Hunting the edges," then, is ungentlemanly behavior, is the opposite of the formal game that a driven hunt with tweeds and gillies represents, is, finally, straddling the balance point of clapboard and forest, reason and instinct, beauty and the beast. What follows is, at last, the final coda, tail-piece, tale feather. Wisconsin hunters of my era may remember from Miss Swan's weekly singing lesson in the State Graded School that John Peel broke his neck while harrying foxes with his horse and hounds. Good hunting!

Blood Sport

Walking some road I saw
a self-made mobile: geese.
Carousing carousel
with woodwind-reedy organ,
they sailed like heavy leaves,
clockwise but horizontal,
above white cockle and hoary alyssum,
down, then away.
The heron, ruffled, goose-roused
angled with snake-slant sideling neck
away, across to anyone's cornfield-lake
(it's been a rainy season),
spread its dusk-feathered, dark, winged robe
and stilled above the stiller pond.

Man-made mobiles are dross:
they hang from strings.
These pumping hearts, pure pulse,
bring beauty without thought of beauty.
Foraging, merest survival—see!—
can outsing art and criticism too.

A scholar's recent text *From a View to a Death*
chants "D'ye ken John Peel" but then defines
all chase as rape.
No. It is love, is that same singular fate
that pricks the hoary hunter
on to the hoarse "Halloa!",
identity with the ceaseless wheel of the geese,
the stillness of that great, flat beak
in every pool.
He may not be mere thought,
but needs must miss or catch his meat
and dress it, too:

live like the white-cheeked geese,
and goitered, louring heron,
chase, catch, or lose, then lie—a heavy leaf—
under white cockle and hoary alyssum,
but do, and do, and do.

October 1993

Acknowledgments

Acknowledgments

All illustrations are woodcuts by Thomas W. Nason, provided by Janet W. Eltinge.

Excerpts from Aldo Leopold, *A Sand County Almanac* (New York: Oxford University Press, 1949), p. 54. Copyright © 1949 Oxford University Press. Reprinted with the permission of Oxford University Press.

Excerpt from *This Incomperable Lande*. Copyright © 1989 by Thomas J. Lyon. Reprinted by permission of Houghton Mifflin Company. All rights reserved.

Excerpt from "Avoiding News by the River," a poem by W. S. Merwin. From *The Lice* (New York: Atheneum, 1967). Copyright 1963, 1964, 1965, 1966, 1967 by W. S. Merwin. All rights reserved.

Excerpt from E. B. Michell, *The Art and Practice of Hawking* (Newton, Mass.: C. T. Branford, 1960).

Excerpts from "Field and Stream" and "Adorning the Buckhorn Helmet" by Jerald Bullis. From *Adorning the Buckhorn Helmet* (Ithaca, N.Y.: Ithaca House, 1976). Reprinted by permission of Catherine Latham.

Excerpt from Frank L. Beebe, *A Falconry Manual* (Blaine, Wash.: Hancock House, 1984).

"Blood Sport" first published in *Oasis, a Literary Magazine*, July/September 1994; "Blow in Her Ear" first published in *Fins and Feathers* (Ohio), November 1986, reprinted in *Wisconsin Outdoor Journal: Wisconsin Hunting '94*, September 1994; a shortened version of "Dave's Buck" appeared in *North American Whitetail*, July 1996, under the title "A Buck for the Baseball Player"; "Esther's Ducks" first published in *Wisconsin Outdoor Journal*, August 1996; "Fall Tree" first published in *Oasis, a Literary Magazine*, July/September 1994; "First Goose" first published in *Wisconsin Sportsman*, November/December 1986; "Hunting with the Farmer" first published in *RGS: The Ruffed Grouse Society Magazine*, September/October 1994; "Hunting with a Poet" first published in *RGS: The Ruffed Grouse Society Magazine*, November/December 1995; "Jakes" first published in modified form in *The Turkey Hunter*, October/November 1992; "Listen to the Quiet" first published in *Wisconsin Outdoor Journal: Wisconsin Hunting '95*, September 1995; "The No. 8 Hook!" first published in *MidWest Outdoors*, January 1989; "The Pipes, the Pipes Are Calling" first published in *Wisconsin Sportsman*, November/December 1984; "The Real Buck" first published as "Afternoons in the Real World," *Wisconsin West*, November 1994; "The Running of the

Deer" first published as "Bringing Down the Buck," *The Milwaukee Journal Magazine: The Wisconsin Deer Hunter,* November 13, 1994; "Thrum-Whoosh" first published in *Wisconsin Outdoor Journal,* December 1992; "Thy Neighbor's Pheasant" first published in *Wisconsin Sportsman,* September/October 1984; "Two Hunters and a Fool" first published in *Gray's Sporting Journal,* Winter 1988; "Up North" first published in *Wisconsin Outdoor Journal: Fishing '94,* Spring 1994.